Your First Chess Lessons

Paul van der Sterren

T0153477

First published in the UK by Gambit Publications Ltd 2016

Copyright © Paul van der Sterren 2016

ISBN-13: 978-1-910093-95-5
ISBN-10: 1-910093-95-5

DISTRIBUTION:
Worldwide (except USA): Central Books Ltd, 50 Freshwater Road, Chadwell Heath, London RM8 1RX, England.
Tel +44 (0)20 8986 4854 Fax +44 (0)20 8533 5821.
E-mail: orders@Centralbooks.com

Gambit Publications Ltd, 50 Freshwater Road, Chadwell Heath, London RM8 1RX, England.
E-mail: info@gambitbooks.com
Website (regularly updated): www.gambitbooks.com

Edited by Graham Burgess
Typeset by John Nunn
Cover illustration by Shane D. Mercer
Printed in the USA by Bang Printing, Brainerd, Minnesota

10 9 8 7 6 5 4 3 2 1

Gambit Publications Ltd
Directors: Dr John Nunn GM, Murray Chandler GM, and Graham Burgess FM
German Editor: Petra Nunn WFM

Contents

Introduction

Chess is one of the oldest games known to mankind and its devotees can be found all over the world. It can be played for fun, for the excitement of winning and for a thousand other reasons. It is a game so rich and complicated that no human has ever played it to perfection (nor has a computer!), yet the rules are fairly straightforward and can be learned in under an hour.

Part 1 of this book will be devoted to explaining those rules. Once the reader has understood them, he will be able to play chess.

Part 2 consists of a number of lessons which will take the reader step by step through the main elements of the strategy and tactics of the game, explaining also the vocabulary that comes with reading a chess book. A few simple exercises are included at the end of each lesson. These are intended to help the reader make the transition from merely reading about chess to actually thinking about it, an important step in what is after all a thinking game.

Armed with this knowledge, those of my readers who want to deepen their understanding will be able to explore the extremely rich and varied body of chess literature and find out for themselves which books or Internet sites could be of further use to them.

The potential for such deepening of understanding is immense. 'Chess is a sea in which a gnat may drink and an elephant may bathe' according to an old proverb of unknown origin. It is one of the great attractions of chess that there will always be room for improvement, even for the mightiest of elephants.

But let us consider ourselves gnats to begin with and start drinking...

Part 1: The Rules

Lesson 1: The Board and the Pieces

Chess is played on a chessboard. There are two players, who each have 16 chess pieces at the start of the game. The chessboard looks like this:

The board is a square consisting of 8 by 8 smaller squares of alternating dark and light colour. We call these 'dark squares' and 'light squares'. In printed diagrams they are black and white, whereas on wooden boards they may be dark brown and light brown, while plastic boards tend to be green and cream or brown and cream.

The right way to place the board is with a light square in the bottom right-hand corner of both players (i.e. 'light on the right').

In the same way the pieces are called white and black, though in reality their colours may also be light and dark brown respectively, just like the squares of the board. The two sides are called White and Black once the game starts, though in their case with capital letters.

The 16 pieces with which each player starts the game are divided
as follows:

1	King	♔
1	Queen	♕
2	Rooks	♖♖
2	Bishops	♗♗
2	Knights	♘♘
8	Pawns	♙♙♙♙♙♙♙♙

At the start of the game the pieces are placed on the board like
this:

Note that the position is symmetrical apart from the kings and
queens. The queens both go 'on their own colour': that is, the white
queen on a light square and the black queen on a dark square.

Diagrams are normally given with the white pieces at the bottom
and the black pieces at the top. Starting from this position, White and
Black alternately make a move until the game is over. Making a
move is compulsory; the rules of chess do not allow a player to
'pass'. White always makes the first move.

Now how does 'making a move' work? It means moving one of
your own pieces from one square to another square. White can only
move white pieces, while Black can only move black pieces. A piece
can move to an empty square or to a square where a piece of the opposite side (an 'enemy piece') is standing. The latter is called *capturing* or *taking* a piece. The piece that is being moved goes to the
square where the enemy piece stood, which is then removed from the
board. There can never be more than one piece on a single square.

Every type of piece has its own unique way of moving. Let us look at each of the pieces in turn.

The King

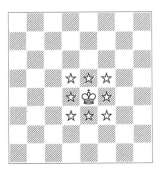

The king is the most important piece in the game and we will examine its unique role more fully in a moment. Strangely enough though, its range of movement is very limited. The king may move to any square adjacent to the one it is standing on, whether the movement is horizontal, vertical or diagonal, but no further. The above diagram shows a king with its maximum range of 8 possible squares, all of them freely accessible. Should there be another piece standing on any of these squares, then the king may capture it if it is an enemy piece, but if it is one of his own pieces, that square is inaccessible.

In the left-hand diagram, the king may move to all of the squares that were available in the previous diagram, except to the square on which the bishop is standing.

In the right-hand diagram the white king may (but does not have to) capture the black pawn. Capturing is not compulsory in chess; it is optional.

The Queen

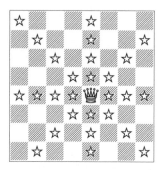

Once again, the stars indicate which squares the queen could move to – as you can see, it has a far wider range than the king! The queen can move *horizontally, vertically or diagonally* in a straight line, forwards or backwards, and *any number of squares* (rather than the king's one-square hop). In the above diagram the queen may move to a total of 27 different squares. However, if another piece is standing on one or more of these lines, the way for the queen is blocked: it cannot move beyond another piece – despite its great power, the queen doesn't jump!

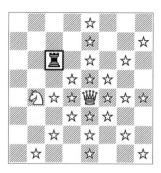

The queen cannot go to or beyond the square where its own knight is standing. Likewise, the squares beyond the black rook have become inaccessible, but the queen may capture the black rook.

The Rook

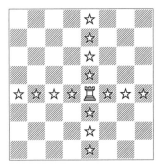

The rook is a powerful piece, but less mobile than the queen: it moves along vertical and horizontal lines, but not along diagonals. Just like the queen, the rook is restricted in its movement if another piece is standing in its way, whether this is a white or a black piece, though it may capture an enemy piece.

The Bishop

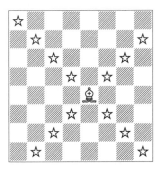

The bishop moves along diagonals only. This means that a bishop can never move from a light square to a dark square or vice versa. The bishop that starts the game on a light square will remain on light squares until it is captured or the game ends and the same is true for a bishop starting on a dark square. The bishop is restricted in its movements in the same way as are queen and rook: it cannot jump over another piece, but it may capture an enemy piece.

The Knight

 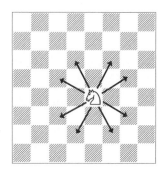

The movement of the knight differs greatly from that of all other pieces. While the queen, rook and bishop may move as far as they like (or can) along their vertical, horizontal or diagonal lines, the knight has no choice how far it will go and does not move along a straight line at all. But what really sets the knight apart is the fact that it jumps *over* other pieces. It cannot be obstructed in the way other pieces can. Its movement is best understood from diagrams like the above. You will often see the knight's move described as "two squares horizontally and then one square vertically" (etc.), but the point is that the knight does not *go* along this route. The knight simply *jumps* from one square to another. Its route cannot be blocked because it *has* no route – it is more a teleport than a journey!

Online chess: Find an Internet site that broadcasts live games from top-level events, preferably with video and commentary. See how the players conduct themselves at the board and watch them making their decisions.

As is clear from the above diagrams, the maximum number of squares for the knight is 8. If a knight gets close to the edge of the board this number diminishes, since some of its possible squares then start falling outside the chessboard.

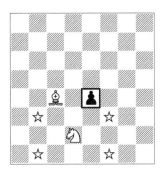 

In the left-hand position the knight has 5 possible moves. There are 4 empty squares available and there is one square where the knight may capture the black pawn.

When the knight stands on a corner square its scope is limited to just 2 squares. In the right-hand diagram it is even further obstructed by its own rook, so the only possible move for the knight here is capturing the black bishop.

The Pawn

Finally we get to the 8 pawns which both White and Black have at the start of the game. Not only their large number, but also their very limited scope for movement reminds us of their humble origins. Chess is believed to have been originally conceived as a war simulation. All the other pieces are either royalty or high-ranking officers, while the pawns are foot-soldiers: ordinary people, fit to serve but not to command. This 'class distinction' is still visible in chess terminology today, for although

Online chess: Find a site where you can play chess over the Internet. Many sites are free to join, or have a free trial membership. Play some games, ideally against players of a similar standard to yourself. Don't be discouraged if you lose a lot of games at first. Try quick games and longer games.

we have so far called all the chessmen 'pieces', chess-players actually exclude pawns from this qualification. The word 'piece' is used for all chessmen *except* the pawns. Pawns are just pawns.

Chess terminology also distinguishes between *major* pieces (queen and rooks) and *minor* pieces (knights and bishops). The king stands alone and above this distinction.

Nevertheless, as we are about to see, the pawn has some very interesting features of its own, one of which can even be called astonishing.

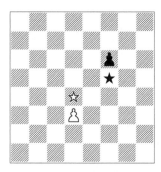

The standard move of a pawn is to go one step forward (viewed from its own side of the board). That is a very small range of action indeed, far smaller than that of any of the *pieces*. But there are two exceptions to this basic movement which make a lot of difference. To begin with, when a pawn is still on its original square (i.e. it has not moved in the game so far) and its way forward is unobstructed, it may move one *or two* squares forward, as in the left-hand diagram below.

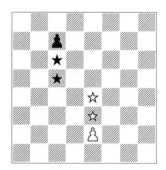

Secondly, the pawn is the only chess piece that *captures* in an altogether different way from its normal movement. If its way forward is blocked, the pawn has no moves. In the right-hand diagram neither pawn can move. Their path ahead is barred, and pawns cannot move backwards.

But if there is an enemy piece (or a pawn) on the square *diagonally* in front of the pawn, that piece (or pawn) may be *captured*.

In the left-hand position the white pawn cannot *move* directly forward, but it can *take* either of the black pawns diagonally opposed to it. Should White decide to take the pawn on the left, the resulting position would be the one shown in the right-hand diagram.

And as if all this were not strange enough, there is one weird exception to these rules.

If you have understood the above, you will agree that if the black pawn moved *one* square forward, it could then be taken by the white pawn. This much is clear and easy to understand. Now, you will notice the black pawn is still on its original square, and could therefore move *two* squares forward, as we saw on page 12. However, if it did so, *it could be captured by the enemy pawn in exactly the same way as if it had only advanced one square.*

Confused? The next two diagrams should make this odd rule clearer.

In the left-hand diagram, the black pawn has just moved two squares forward. On his next move, White can choose to capture it with his pawn *as if* it had only moved forward *one* square. This would then result in the position shown in the right-hand diagram.

The black pawn has disappeared and the white pawn has landed on exactly the same square where it would be if the black pawn had moved just *one* square forward and been taken *there*.

This is called taking *en passant*, which is French for 'in passing'. It is permitted *only* on the very next move.

Over-the-board chess: Find a chess club in your area. This might be at your school or workplace, or your town's chess club. Playing real opponents face-to-face feels very different from playing online, and you'll learn a lot from talking to your opponents after the games.

It is not allowed to postpone the *en passant* capture until a more convenient moment. It must be done either at once or not at all.

But the most spectacular aspect of the pawn by far is what happens when it reaches the far side of the board.

If in the left-hand position the pawn moves forward, it is *promoted* to a white piece of White's choosing. The pawn stops being a pawn and starts its new life as a piece automatically and as part of the same move. This is called 'promotion' or 'pawn promotion'. The pawn changes into a queen, rook, bishop or knight (but not into a king!) even when White still has all his original pieces. It is perfectly possible for a player to have, for instance, two queens, three rooks or four bishops (though the latter two are highly uncommon!).

The player who promotes a pawn does not have to do anything special for this, except to replace the original pawn with his chosen piece. The position after promotion to a queen (which is called 'queening') is shown in the right-hand diagram.

Pawn promotion is also possible by *capturing* an enemy piece.

In the left-hand position the white pawn cannot move directly forward since there is a black rook standing in its way, but it can capture the other rook, which results in promotion. If a queen is chosen, the resulting position is shown in the right-hand diagram.

Castling

Finally, there is one move which falls outside all 'regular' movements we have seen so far and which is no less strange than the *en passant* capture or the promotion of a pawn, though of an entirely different nature. It is called *castling*.

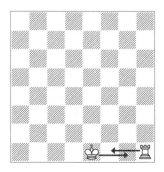

Castling is a combined move by a king and a rook (of the same colour). In the left-hand diagram above, White may *castle*, providing three conditions are met (we will discuss them shortly). In order to castle, White moves his king two squares towards the rook and then the rook 'jumps' over the king, so that it lands on the square next to the king – see the right-hand diagram.

This is called castling kingside (or sometimes 'castling short'). Castling queenside (or 'castling long') is also possible and it goes like this:

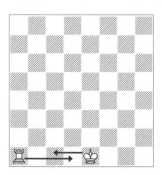
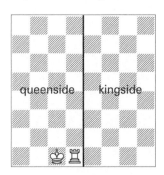

In the left-hand position White may castle queenside. Again the king moves two squares towards the rook – in this case to the left. As before, the rook jumps over the king, in this case going three squares to the right. The right-hand diagram shows the resulting position.

The term 'kingside' indicates the side of the board where the two kings stand at the start of the game, while 'queenside' means the side where the queens are in the starting position (which we saw on page 6).

Now what are the three conditions that have to be met in order to make castling possible?

First, neither the king nor the rook involved may have previously moved. If, for instance, the king moves to its left and then back again to its original square, castling is no longer possible. If one of the rooks has previously moved and then returned to its original square, castling with this rook is no longer possible, but castling in the other direction remains legal, providing of course that *that* rook has not previously moved.

Secondly, castling is not allowed in a position where the king is in *check*. Check is a very important element of chess, closely connected with the king's unique role in the game, which we shall examine more fully in the next lesson. A king is said to be in check when it is *threatened with capture* (and by now we know how each of the pieces captures, including the pawn's odd diagonal capture). A king in check *must* get out of the check immediately. Remaining in check or stepping into another check is not allowed.

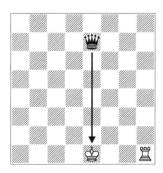

In this position the white king is in check, for it is threatened by the black queen. White can potentially defend against this threat in several ways: the king can move aside, the attacking piece may be captured, another white piece may *interpose* between the white king and the black queen, but one thing that is *not* allowed is castling.

This rule applies to the king only. When the rook involved in the castling is under attack, castling remains legal.

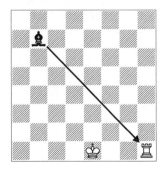 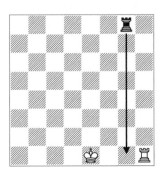

In the left-hand position, the white rook is under attack, yet castling is allowed.

We have already said that a king *cannot move into check*, so it follows that castling is not allowed if the king would be in check on the square where it would stand after castling. But the trickiest of the three conditions is that a king cannot even *pass through* a square where it *would* be in check *if* it stood there (which in actual fact it never does because it only passes through). This rule is sometimes expressed as 'you can't castle *through* check or into check'.

In the right-hand diagram above, castling kingside is not allowed for the white king would then be in check. A king can never move into check.

 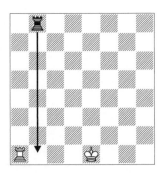

In the left-hand position, castling queenside is not allowed for the white king would then *pass through* a square where it would be in check. Again, this rule applies to the king only. If the *rook* needs to pass through a square where it would be under attack, castling remains perfectly possible.

Look at the right-hand diagram. In order to castle queenside, the white rook has to pass through a square where it would be attacked. This is allowed. White can castle queenside if he wants to.

You now know how all the pieces move. Congratulations! However, this is still not quite enough to be able to play a full game of chess, as there are some additional rules you need to learn – including the small matter of the actual aim of the game itself! We shall cover them in the next lesson. For now, please make sure that you are very familiar with the moves of the pieces. Practise them on your chessboard, and maybe get a friend to test you on them. I have also provided a few exercises below, to check your knowledge of some of the trickier points.

Exercises

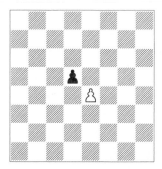

1) Look at this position both from White's point of view and from Black's. What moves are possible?

2) Suppose that, in the previous diagram, it is Black to move and he moves his pawn forward, resulting in this position. Can White then capture the pawn *en passant*?

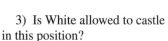

3) Is White allowed to castle in this position?

4) Is White allowed to castle in this position?

All solutions are to be found on page 90 at the end of this book.

Emanuel Lasker, José Capablanca and Alexander Alekhine
Generally considered the greatest players from the pre-WW2 era, these three champions reigned over the chess world for half a century. Emanuel Lasker (1868-1941) was born in Germany and held the title of World Champion for a record 27 years, from 1894 to 1921. His play was marked by great tenacity and smart psychology. His successor, José Raúl Capablanca (1888-1942) from Cuba, was legendary for his ease and elegance of play and for his near-invincibility. When he *was* finally defeated in a match for the title in 1927 by Russian-born Alexander Alekhine (1892-1946), this shocked the chess world. Alekhine's play was characterized by brilliant combinations and by a fierce will to win. He lost the title to Max Euwe in 1935, regained it in 1937 and then kept it until his death, the only world champion ever to do so.

Lesson 2: The Aim of the Game

Check and Checkmate

When explaining the rules of castling in the previous lesson, we briefly touched upon the important topic of *check*. This means that there is a direct threat to capture the king. When a player's king is in check, he *must* get out of the check immediately. But what happens if he can't? This brings us to the very essence of the game of chess, for if he can't, then it's *checkmate* (often shortened to 'mate') and the game is over.

The aim of the game is to capture the enemy king, but unlike the other pieces, the king is never actually taken. When the king is in check and there is no way out of the check, it is checkmate and that is good enough. Checkmate ends the game immediately and automatically.

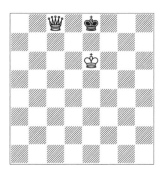 

For example, in the left-hand position, the black king is under attack from the white queen and does not have a single move to get out of the check. It cannot move to a square next to the white king, and otherwise it cannot escape the check from the queen. Thus it is checkmate and Black has lost the game.

In the right-hand position the black king is in check but is not checkmated, for Black has several ways to cover the check. It is true that the king still has no legal moves, but Black has three options: he can interpose his rook between his king and the white queen, or he can capture the white queen, both with his knight and with his bishop.

In theory, checkmating the enemy king is the only way to win, but in practice – and especially in games between experienced players – there are several other ways for a game to be won and lost, some of which occur far more frequently than an actual checkmate.

First, a player may decide to *resign*. An experienced player will normally know when all hope of saving an inferior position has become futile and at some point he may decide that resignation makes more sense than prolonging the agony. If, for instance, a player sees that he will be checkmated by force in two or three more moves, he will usually not wait for the inevitable to happen and he will resign straight away. Heavy material losses will normally also cause a player to resign. As we shall see in Part 2 of this book, not every piece has the same value and the material balance may become so thoroughly disrupted that the battle becomes a wholly unequal one.

It is important to note, though, that resignation is never obligatory. It is just a tool for an experienced player to end a struggle that has become hopeless. This is a purely personal decision and one that can never be enforced.

A third way to win (or rather to lose) occurs when a game is played with a chess clock. In an official tournament or any other form of competitive chess, a clock will always be used, but even in informal games, players often prefer to use a clock to add some extra excitement or to make sure that the game does not last too long. Many types of time-limits are possible, especially with electronic clocks, which are standard nowadays. It could be a set amount of time for the whole game (for instance, five minutes or one hour), or it could be a more intricate form of time-limit like 90 minutes for the first 35 moves followed by 15 minutes for the rest of the game. The chess clock registers the time used by both players. If a player exceeds the time-limit, then he has '*lost on time*', regardless of the actual position on the board. Even if you are three pieces up or if you are about to deliver checkmate, exceeding the time-limit will lose you the game. Clocks know no mercy.

Nowadays there are additional ways to lose a tournament game. For instance it is no longer allowed to carry a mobile phone with you while playing in a tournament. This is not just because a phone ringing would disturb other players, but to prevent various forms of cheating, such as consulting a chess 'engine' on a smartphone. The World Chess Federation, called FIDE (Fédération Internationale des Échecs), has introduced a whole series of new rules governing the conduct of players during an official tournament game and the penalty for breaking any of these is usually a forfeit of the game. If you are going to play competitive chess, it is wise to be familiar with the current FIDE rules, and any other rules that are specific to the event in which you are playing. Note that there are often special rules for rapidplay games.

Draw

A game can also be *drawn*. In this case neither player has won, and neither player has lost. Again, this result can be achieved in several ways: stalemate, threefold repetition, the fifty-move rule, by mutual agreement or due to insufficient material.

The most crucial of these is *stalemate*, for this is the only way to draw which is inherent in the game of chess itself. All other ways for a game to end in a draw are of a more practical nature. But stalemate, like checkmate, is one of the basic ingredients of chess. And just like checkmate, stalemate ends the game immediately and automatically.

This diagram differs only marginally from the one on page 21 where the black king was checkmated. The only difference is that the white queen is on a different square.

And yet, provided it is Black to move, this position is a draw, for Black is *stalemated*. There is not a single legal move that he can make, yet his king is not in check so it isn't checkmate. The game has reached a dead end: draw.

Naturally, if it is White to move in this position, there is no problem and the game simply continues; he could in fact give checkmate on his next move in one of two ways (*can you see how?*).

A game can also be drawn if the *same position occurs three times* (known as 'threefold repetition'). It must be *exactly* the same position, with the same player to move and the same 'invisible' possibilities. If one side still has the right to castle the first time the position occurs, but has lost it the second or third time, for example because his king has moved, the position is not identical and there is no threefold repetition. Also, if in the first position an *en passant* capture is possible, there can be no threefold repetition based on that position because the right to capture *en passant* will have evaporated by the time the position occurs a second or third time (see page 14).

A draw by threefold repetition is not automatic, but has to be claimed. In an informal situation this will simply be done by informing the opponent of the fact, who will then either agree or disagree and the game will end or continue accordingly. In a more formal situation, for instance in a tournament game, the player will claim the draw by informing his opponent *or* the arbiter of his *intention* of playing the move that brings about the same position for the third time. If the arbiter is called, he will check the validity of the claim and either declare the game drawn or the claim to be invalid (in which case the game continues with the move that was announced). In a chess tournament, the arbiter has a similar role to the referee, judge or umpire in other sports.

Naturally, this rather formal procedure is not something that a beginner needs to worry about. It is important to note, though, that it is a threefold repetition of the *position* we are talking about. This does not necessarily involve a repetition of *moves*, because it is perfectly possible for the same position to be arrived at by a wholly different set of moves. In practical play this is sometimes overlooked, which often results in a player taken by surprise by his opponent claiming a draw by threefold repetition when he would have dearly liked to play on.

You will often hear people talking about a draw by *perpetual check*. This is a situation where a player can make a series of repeated checks to the enemy king, and neither player sees any good way to break this sequence. In this case, the position will sooner or later be repeated three times and a player will either claim the draw or else the players will *agree* a draw (see below).

The *fifty-move rule* is a rarer way for a game to end in a draw, but important because otherwise a game could go on for ever. If in the last fifty moves ('a move' in this case meaning a move by White *plus* a move by Black) no capture has been made *and* no pawn has been moved, either player is entitled to claim a draw. This normally occurs only in situations where very few pieces are left and where one player has a material advantage that may be enough to win theoretically, but is very difficult to realize in practice. In a case like that the defender, if he manages to survive for fifty moves, is rewarded for his efforts by the possibility of claiming a draw. If the draw is *not* claimed, the game continues as if nothing had happened, but a draw can still be claimed later, provided the conditions of 'no captures and no pawn moves' continue to be met. However, once a player is checkmated or has exceeded the time-limit he loses immediately and automatically and can no longer claim a draw.

A draw can also be *agreed* upon. Basically this is a very simple procedure: one player offers a draw, his opponent accepts, end of game. If the offer is rejected the game simply continues.

Such a 'draw by mutual agreement' is by far the most common way for a game to end in a draw. Sometimes the players agree a draw because there is no realistic scope for the game to end in any other way, and playing further moves would be completely pointless. It is a question of common sense. However, the reasons for agreeing to a draw are not always purely technical. In fact they can be, at least in part, of an emotional and sometimes highly personal nature, and top players are sometimes criticized by their fans for agreeing to a draw too early. On an amateur level though, most people will agree that having to catch a train, feeling tired or even being fed up with the game are perfectly acceptable reasons for agreeing to a draw. Enough is enough.

The correct procedure is to make a move and offer a draw at the same time, before pressing one's clock (if a clock is used). Offering a draw while your opponent is thinking about his move, thereby disrupting his thought process, is considered not just bad form but is even against the rules. Making repeated draw offers is also poor sportsmanship.

There is in fact another way for the game to end in a draw: *insufficient material*. If both players have just a king left, then there is clearly no way for either side to give mate. This is an immediate draw. There are a few other cases of insufficient material that we shall discuss later – see page 52.

And that's it. **You now know the basic rules, and you can play chess.**

But for anyone wanting to know more than just the rules, for anyone who really wants to *understand* chess, the journey is only just beginning. In Part 2 we will take a look at the basic elements of the tactics and strategy of the game. We will also get to know a lot more chess vocabulary, a vital prerequisite for understanding what chess books, magazines and websites are all about.

Exercises

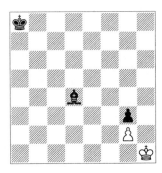

5) Has Black been checkmated here?

6) What is going on in this position if it is White to move?

Part 2: The Basics of Strategy and Tactics

Lesson 3: Chess Notation

So far we have described chess moves in ordinary language, using terms like "the white king moves one square to its right and captures the black bishop". To describe a whole game in this way would quickly get rather tiresome, so we will now take our knowledge of chess terminology a step further and start using proper chess *notation*. There are several notation systems in existence, but we will use the one that is simplest and most common: *algebraic* notation.

As you can see, each square is identified by labelling the horizontal lines (called 'ranks') 1 through 8 from bottom to top and the vertical lines (called 'files') 'a' through 'h' from left to right. White's left bottom corner square is a1, while Black's left bottom corner square (viewed from *his side* of the board) is h8. Thus every square gets a unique code, and these codes do not change based on which player is moving.

On the basis of these coordinates, every move can be noted down as follows: first an uppercase letter for the piece that is being moved, K for king, Q for queen, R for rook, B for bishop, N for knight and ... *nothing* for a pawn, for even in chess notation the old class distinction between officers and common soldiers is still in evidence. Next we simply write the square where the piece is being moved to. Thus a king move from e1 to f1 is noted down as Kf1. A pawn move to e4 is just "e4". When a capture is made, an 'x' is inserted immediately before the destination square. For instance, when a knight goes from e4 to d6 and thereby captures an enemy piece (which piece remains unspecified), this is written down as Nxd6. When two identical pieces can move to the same square, the moving piece is identified by inserting one of the coordinates of the square of departure. For example, when White has knights on c3 and g1, moving one of these knights to e2 is either noted down as Nce2 or Nge2, depending on which knight is moved. Or when Black has two rooks on the a-file, say on a8 and a2, a rook move to a4 becomes either ...R8a4 or ...R2a4. The three dots show that this is a move by Black. For pawn *captures*, the file of departure is always included; e.g., dxe5 for a pawn from d4 capturing on e5.

In case of an *en passant* capture, "e.p." is sometimes added (though this is not essential) and if a pawn promotes, the letter denoting the new piece is added to the notation (e.g. e8Q). For castling, a special code is used: 0-0 for castling kingside and 0-0-0 for castling queenside. It is also customary to add '+' if the move gives check. The origin of this symbol is shrouded in obscurity. A burial cross perhaps to remind the king of the deadly danger he is in? The most standard symbol for checkmate is '#'.

We should note that in chess books, it is normal to use *figurines* for the pieces, and we shall do so for the rest of this book! But note that there is no need for you to draw these little pictures when writing down chess moves by hand! The figurines are very similar to those we have seen in the diagrams in this book so far:

King	=	K	=	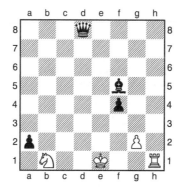
Queen	=	Q	=	
Rook	=	R	=	
Bishop	=	B	=	
Knight	=	N	=	

In official games, players are required to record their moves (generally by writing them down on a *scoresheet*) except when there is a very fast time-limit. This scoresheet is needed for claiming a win if your opponent exceeds the time-limit without having made the required number of moves and for claiming a draw on the grounds of threefold repetition or the fifty-move rule.

Naturally, in informal games no record of the moves is required. Yet the great thing about recording even an unofficial game is that it can thus be analysed, commented upon and stored. As we will have reason to explain later, the whole of chess literature (including websites), is based on the recording of games. Whenever a game is recorded it becomes part of a very rich chess heritage. It will find its place, however modest, in history.

This position allows us to illustrate all sorts of moves and how they are noted down. Let's start with the king: if White moves his king one square up, this is recorded as ♔e2.

If it is Black to move, he might want to move his queen, let's say, to a5. This is recorded as ...♛a5 (or ...♛a5+ for this move is a check).

If White moves his rook, this is recorded as ♖h5 if the rook moves four squares forward, or ♖g1 if it moves one square sideways.

The black bishop can capture the white knight on b1. This is written down as ...♝xb1.

If it is White to move he may want to prevent this by moving his knight away from b1; for instance: ♘c3.

The white pawn on g2 can go one *or* two squares forward. This becomes either g3 or g4 in notation (as already mentioned, the pawn is not given a figurine or an identifying letter). Should White decide to play g4, Black can, if he wishes, capture the white pawn *en passant* with his own pawn on f4. The notation for this move is ...fxg3 (or ...fxg3 e.p.). Note that not only the actual movement of the capturing pawn, but even the notation is as if White's previous move had been g3 (rather than g4, which it actually was): the black pawn ends on g3, so the notation becomes ...fxg3.

Black's pawn on a2 is on the brink of promotion. If it is Black's move, he even has a choice between simply advancing the pawn to a1 or capturing the white knight on b1. In both cases Black has to decide which piece he chooses for the pawn to promote to. His choice will be noted down by adding the symbol for the chosen piece *after* the actual move itself: thus ...a1♕ or ...axb1♕+ if he chooses a queen or, for instance, ...a1♖ or ...axb1♗ if otherwise.

> *Over-the-board chess:* Find a local competition that you can play in, such as a weekend or evening event, or a local league. Playing games where the result really matters will put your nerve and decision-making to a true test. You might even win some money!

Finally, if it is White to move he may castle kingside (assuming that neither the king nor the rook has moved yet). This is written down as 0-0. Castling queenside (if it were possible here) would be 0-0-0. An easy way to remember which is which is that the number of zeroes equals the number of empty squares between king and rook: 2 for kingside castling and 3 for queenside castling.

This system of notation is known as *short* algebraic notation. It has the advantage of taking up very little space and is more or less standard in international publications. Another version of algebraic notation is called *long* algebraic notation. This system includes the square of departure for each move followed by a hyphen. Thus, in the previous diagram the move ♔f1 becomes ♔e1-f1 in long notation, ...♗xb1 changes into ...♗f5xb1, g4 becomes g2-g4 and ...fxg3 becomes ...f4xg3. Both systems are allowed in official games. In this book we will use short algebraic notation.

There is one standard feature of chess notation that we haven't encountered yet: *move numbers*. These indicate on which move of the game a move was played. The first move gets a number '1' before it, the second move a number '2' and so on. We shall see them in the next lesson, in which we examine some possible lines of play from the starting position.

Bobby Fischer
American grandmaster Robert James Fischer (1943-2008) became World Champion by beating Soviet grandmaster Boris Spassky in a match held in Reykjavik (Iceland) in 1972, which is often referred to as the 'Match of the Century'. Being seen at the time not just as a personal competition, but also as a kind of sportive and intellectual culmination of the Cold War, this match attracted media attention of a magnitude that had never been seen before in the chess world and is unlikely ever to be surpassed. Unfortunately, it marked not only the high point of a truly brilliant career but also the end of it, as Fischer never played in an official tournament or match ever again. He lost his title in 1975, when he was unable to come to an agreement with FIDE on the conditions for a match against his official challenger, Anatoly Karpov.

Lesson 4: The First Obstacles

Now that we know not only the rules of chess but the notation as well, we can proceed to what is often termed the 'technique' of the game. How do the rules (which after all are nothing but words on paper) translate into a real game of chess? What is needed for winning a game and what must be avoided? Let us therefore simply start a game and see what problems we encounter while playing.

From here onwards it is advisable to have a real chessboard in front of you while reading this book and physically execute each move that is mentioned. In order to become thoroughly acquainted with chess it is necessary not just to familiarize your thought-processes, but also your *hands* with the actual playing of moves. Reading about chess is fine, but experiencing what it feels like to make a move is better.

I hope you remember the starting position (we saw it earlier in the book), but here it is again:

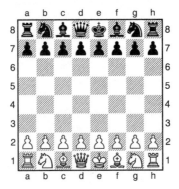

One of the basic characteristics of the starting position is that almost all of the pieces are blocked in. Only the knights can move, and even they have just two possible destination squares: White's knight on g1 can move to f3 or h3, while the knight on b1 can move to c3 or a3. On the other hand, all the pawns enjoy their maximum freedom of movement, as they can all move forward one or two squares. Thus it should come as no surprise that the majority of chess games start with a pawn move.

1 e4

As soon as we start discussing moves in a specific position (e.g. the starting position) rather than in general terms, a move number is added to the notation. Thus when the first move is to advance the pawn from e2 to e4, this is noted down as 1 e4 (or 1 e2-e4 in long notation).

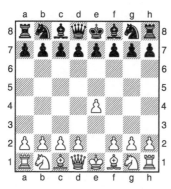

Position after 1 e4
Black to move

1 e4 and 1 d4 are the most popular first moves. Both moves have the advantage that they open up lines for a bishop and the queen while they also give White a foothold in what is called the *centre* of the board, meaning the four squares e4, d4, e5 and d5. The centre is an area of *strategic importance*, especially in the opening stages of a game, for this is often where the two armies first make contact and where the fighting breaks out.

1...d5

Whenever a move by Black is noted down separately (i.e. without the preceding move by White) we place three dots between the number and the actual notation of the move in order to

Online chess: Follow a high-level event online, trying to understand each move played. While each player is thinking, try to work out what move they are going to play. You can also check your ideas against the computer assessments that many online chess broadcasts feature.

distinguish it from a move by White. This is done to avoid confusion. In a sentence like "37 ♘g5 was a really bad move", it is important that the reader should understand that it is a move by *White* that is being talked about. Had this been a move by Black, the notation would have read "37...♘g5".

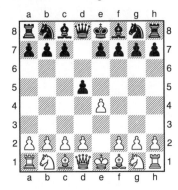

Position after 1...d5
White to move

Black also opens up lines for his pieces that are blocked in on the back rank. A *rank*? Yes, in chess terminology a horizontal line is called a rank and a vertical one is a file. Thus we speak of the a-*file* and the e-*file*, but of the first *rank* and the seventh *rank*. The first and eighth ranks are also called *back ranks* if specifically mentioned from either White's or Black's point of view. The first rank is White's back rank, while the eighth rank is Black's back rank.

Note that when we talk of 'lines' in a general sense (e.g., as in 'open lines'), we can mean ranks, files and diagonals.

In chess literature, many sequences of initial moves have been given names. This particular *opening* (a word that is used to denote the starting phase of a game) is called the Scandinavian Defence or simply 'the Scandinavian'. The term 'defence' is purely conventional and implies that the defining move of this opening is made by Black, who is *supposed* to be the defender when the game starts. This is due to the fact that it is White who makes the first move, so White is supposed to hold (or to take) the *initiative*. Whether Black (or White) is *really* attacking or defending makes no difference for deciding whether an opening should be called a 'defence' rather than an 'opening'.

The 'initiative' is best defined as 'the ability to create threats'. It is an important feature of chess strategy, and generally a very useful thing to possess, though not quite the same thing as having an *advantage*.

In this case Black clearly isn't defending, because 1...d5 attacks White's pawn on e4 and if anything this deserves to be called an aggressive move, rather than a defensive one. Still, an attacker should always bear in mind that the enemy can strike too.

2 exd5

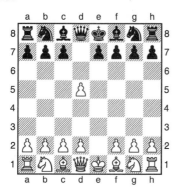

Position after 2 exd5
Black to move

Pawns *move* in a straight line forward, but *capture* diagonally forward. White has now won a pawn, so for the moment, he is a pawn ahead. But Black is able to redress the material balance at once.

2...♛xd5

The black pawn that stood on d5 was *protected* by the black queen. Black has now regained his pawn, and the material balance is restored.

3 ♘c3

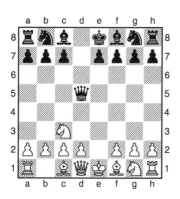

Position after 3 ♘c3
Black to move

The battle is heating up. White's knight on c3 is threatening to capture Black's queen. What can Black do about this?

3...♛e5+

Black's only defence is to move his queen away from the square where it was threatened to another square where it is safe. If we look up this position in chess opening literature (or in a database) we will find that the most popular moves are 3...♛a5, 3...♛d6 and 3...♛d8. These are what are called the *main lines* of the Scandinavian, which means that they are considered the best options for Black by a majority of chess-players. The '*theory*' of the Scandinavian, meaning the segment of chess literature that deals with this particular subject, is largely based on these main lines.

But 3...♛e5+ is also a tempting move, because it is *check*. What should White do now?

4 ♗e2

The king itself cannot move, since on e2, its only available square, it would still be in check. So White has to *interpose* a piece between his king and the black queen. 4 ♛e2, 4 ♘ce2 and 4 ♘ge2 were also possible.

4...♗g4

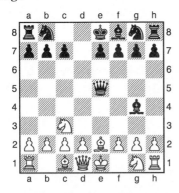

Position after 4...♗g4
White to move

Again Black chooses an aggressive move. He is taking advantage of the white bishop on e2 (the *light-squared bishop*) being 'pinned' in order to place his own light-squared bishop on a square where it would normally be liable to capture (♗xg4).

Whenever a piece is hampered in its freedom of movement because it is either not *allowed* to move (which is the case here: the king can never be exposed to check) or when moving the piece is inadvisable because another piece standing behind it would then lose its cover and be captured, we say this piece is 'pinned'. In this case, White's bishop on e2 is *pinned* against the king so it cannot move.

5 ♘f3

This move is aimed at chasing the black queen away from e5, for on f3 the white knight threatens to capture the queen. This is a perfectly sound plan in itself, but the execution of it isn't flawless. White would have been better advised to play 5 d4, a move that also attacks the black queen, but doesn't have any *positional* drawbacks. The term 'positional' pervades the whole of chess literature. It is used to denote a non-materialistic assessment of either a move or a position rather than a purely materialistic one (i.e. simply counting the pieces and pawns). In this case the 'positional drawback' of White's move 5 ♘f3 is laid bare by Black's reply.

5...♗xf3

Black eliminates an enemy knight. Should White now not be able to recapture, we would have spoken of his loss being a *material* one: he would have been 'a piece down'. But that is not the case here.

6 gxf3

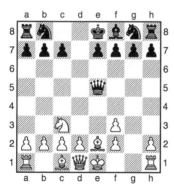

Position after 6 gxf3
Black to move

Assuming a knight and bishop to be of more or less the same value (a subject about which we will have more to say in the next lesson) White has regained his piece, thus restoring the material balance. But he now has '*doubled isolated* pawns' on f2 and f3, and it is these which constitute the positional drawback I was talking about. Two pawns of the same colour that are on the same file are called *doubled* pawns. This very often implies a loss of mobility, since one of them will always be in the other's way. Pawns that have no friendly pawns on the neighbouring files are called *isolated* pawns. This means that they cannot be defended by other pawns and that the square in front of them would be an excellent location for an enemy piece, as it would be hard to dislodge. Thus they are *weak pawns* and there are some *weak squares* around them.

It is important to know, though, that considerations like these present only a guideline. There are countless positions where doubled pawns are actually a tower of strength, and even doubled isolated pawns may not prove to be any real weakness, especially when they allow their pieces to move freely around them. Nevertheless this is a *good* guideline and the position that is under scrutiny here is no exception, as we are about to see.

Everyone who is learning chess has got to rely on guidelines in order to create a minimum of order in the chaos which chess must be to one who is only just starting to penetrate its secrets. With increasing experience comes a more thorough understanding, which will cause guidelines like this to recede into the background. In fact, this is exactly what the learning process in chess is all about: to start seeing the exceptions to every guideline.

6...e6

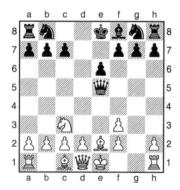

Position after 6...e6
White to move

Again Black opens up a diagonal, this time for his dark-squared bishop. This type of move, which is aimed at mobilizing pieces which are as yet dormant, is called a *developing* move. Both players need to develop the potential of their pieces by giving them scope. The initial position is a perfect example of a situation where almost every piece needs to be developed in order to have an impact (this is another guideline and again a very good one). Developing your pieces is of crucial importance in the opening stages of a game and it can safely be said that whoever does this better is likely to emerge from the opening with the superior position.

7 0-0

White castles and in doing so unpins his bishop on e2. Unfortunately, the move also has a huge drawback that far outweighs this minor advantage. 7 d4! would have been a much better move. By chasing away Black's queen from its dominant position in the centre, while simultaneously opening a useful diagonal for the bishop on c1 and creating a firm outpost in the centre, White would have accomplished three useful short-term strategic aims.

Moves that are assessed as 'weak' or 'bad' are usually given a '?' in chess literature or even a '??' if they are *very* weak. Likewise, a 'good' or 'strong' move can be given an '!' or even '!!'. In this case I would certainly add at least one question mark to White's last move and probably two: 7 0-0??.

These symbols are added to the notation of a move when *annotating* a game only (that is, writing up a commentary to the game afterwards). Writing them on your scoresheet during play is definitely not OK and might be seen as a way of trying to annoy or distract the opponent.

7...♗d6!

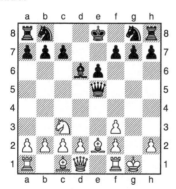

Position after 7...♗d6!
White to move

A very good move and the only way to take advantage of White's mistake. Black is now threatening mate on h2, which is a way of saying that every 'normal' move (like 8 d4) is now met by 8...♕xh2#. If White's pawns on the *kingside* weren't so *weak*, he would be able to parry this threat easily. But as it is, he can only prevent the checkmate by taking some drastic countermeasures which involve rather heavy material losses.

8 f4

Blocking the diagonal between e5 and h2 while attacking the black queen. But...

8...♛xf4

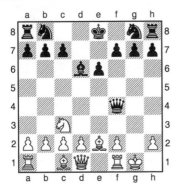

Position after 8...♛xf4
White to move

By capturing the white pawn on f4, Black has simultaneously warded off the threat against his queen and won a pawn, while renewing the threat of checkmate on h2. But White now has a defence against this threat which he did not have when his pawn on f3 was still there.

9 ♗b5+

Check! Black *must* get out of the check so he has no time to checkmate the white king.

9...c6

With this pawn move Black defends against the check and simultaneously attacks the white bishop on b5. There were several other moves to get out of the check (9...♘d7, 9...♘c6, 9...♚f8, 9...♚e7 and 9...♚d8), but by playing 9...c6 Black makes optimal use of the specific features of the position. White

Chess study: Find a chess study partner of a similar level to yourself and with similar interests. This might be someone from your chess club or that you have played online. Exchange analysis and ideas with them, and play friendly and training games. Discuss books and websites that you have found useful.

now has to cope with two threats: the mate on h2 and the attack against his bishop (10...cxb5). It is impossible to ward off both.

10 ♕h5

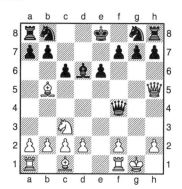

Position after 10 ♕h5
Black to move

The queen now protects h2. By giving up first his pawn on f3 and then his light-squared bishop, White has managed to defend h2, thus preventing the checkmate on h2. But the material loss is a heavy one.

10...♘f6

Black could have taken the bishop on b5 at once, but before he does this he (again) makes use of the concrete possibilities the position offers to bring his king's knight into play 'for free'. Because his queen is now threatened, White has no time to rescue his bishop. This is called a 'gain of tempo'. 'Tempo' is a very old chess term of Italian origin. *Gaining a tempo* is basically getting in a useful extra move for free.

11 ♕h3

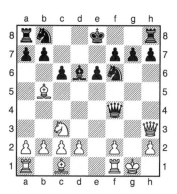

Position after 11 ♕h3
Black to move

White is in trouble and he has to decide what his priorities are. By putting his queen on the h3-square, he continues to protect h2 and also brings his queen to safety. Losing the bishop is of course painful, but far less so than getting checkmated or losing the queen.

It is standard to refer to pieces and pawns in terms of the square they are on. For instance, the 'a1-rook', the 'c6-pawn' and the 'g5-square', etc.

11...cxb5

The opening skirmishes are over and it is safe to say that Black has come out well on top: he has won a pawn and a piece. It is high time for White to try to strike back.

12 ♘xb5

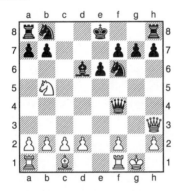

Position after 12 ♘xb5
Black to move

White has captured a pawn that *seems* to have been left undefended. So this looks like a good move. But in chess it is always of vital importance to look at the *whole* picture, i.e. the whole board.

12...♛g5+

With this move Black simultaneously gives check and attacks the white knight on b5. This is called a *double attack* or a *fork*. White has to get his king out of check so he will inevitably lose the knight.

A double attack is a chess *tactic* whereby two enemy targets are attacked at the same time. A fork is a special case of this where one piece creates both threats. A fork can even attack three or more targets, such as a knight giving check while also attacking an enemy queen and rook.

13 ♕g2

Every other queen move (13 ♕g3 or 13 ♕g4) would have been worse for these would have left the queen '*en prise*' (a term borrowed from French; it means that the queen would then have been exposed to capture). White could also have played 13 ♔h1.

13...♕xb5

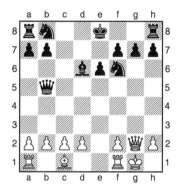

Position after 13...♕xb5
White to move

White is now two pieces down. This constitutes a considerable material handicap. With his next move, he is hoping to reduce the deficit.

14 ♕xg7

The white queen is now threatening both the h8-rook and the f6-knight. One would expect this double attack to result in the win of at least one of these pieces. Unfortunately White has (again) not *calculated* sufficiently deeply. To calculate in chess means to foresee exactly what the results of one's moves should be (assuming good play by both sides). Still, there is only *one* move that exposes the flaw in White's calculations. This is often the case in chess. One player makes a mistake, but there is only one way to punish him and if the opponent does not find it, the game continues as if nothing had happened.

A move like 14 ♕xg7 is called a 'tactical' error, as opposed to a move like 5 ♘f3 which was a mistake of a

Computer chess:
Download a chess *engine* and a *user-interface*. There are some good free ones, but you might prefer to buy them. This enables you to play practice games – but be warned that they are very strong opponents! – and to get the computer's assessments of interesting games that you have seen or played.

positional nature. 12 ♘xb5 was also a tactical error. These are moves that may not be bad 'in themselves' (i.e. there is nothing wrong with them in a positional sense), but which overlook one tactical detail that changes the evaluation of the move completely.

   14...♖g8

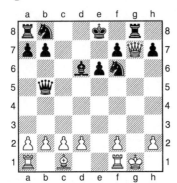

Position after 14...♖g8
White to move

Thus Black not only manages to save his rook (it is now on a square where it is protected by the f6-knight), but he also pins the white queen. As a result, the f6-knight is now also safe and – even more importantly – the white queen is suddenly doomed, for it cannot bring itself into safety by leaving the g-file because of the pin against the king. The best White can do is to get a rook for his queen by playing 15 ♕xg8+, but after 15...♘xg8 White's material losses have become so heavy that an experienced player may well decide to resign at this point (if he had not already done so after 7...♗d6 or 12...♕g5+).

As we have already discussed, resigning is an entirely personal decision. Every player is free to carry on playing as long as he likes. But as an instructional example we are now done with this game, so 'we' shall resign at this point and move on to the next chapter.

Exercises

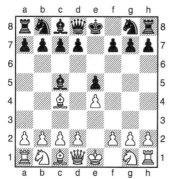

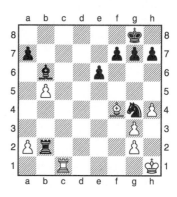

7) A mere two moves have been played: 1 e4 e5 2 ♗c4 ♗c5. Both sides have brought a bishop into play. White now has two different ways of threatening mate. Which two moves am I talking about?

8) In this position Black went for 1...♖xa2. Why was this *not* a good move?

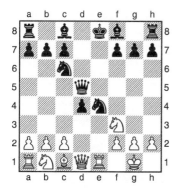

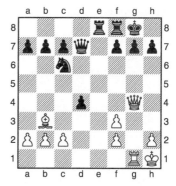

9) Things are not looking too good for White. He is a piece and a pawn down. But could 1 ♘c3 save him?

10) White to play. What is the best move?

Lesson 5: The Relative Value of the Pieces

One of the difficulties that we encountered in the previous lesson was knowing the relative value of different pieces. Is it such a problem if I 'exchange' a queen for a rook? Does it really matter if I am two or three pieces down? And what is more valuable, a knight or a rook? A bishop or three pawns?

It is part of what makes chess such a fascinating game that there is no categorical answer to any of these questions. The value of different pieces depends to a large extent on the peculiarities of the position. Every positional detail has to be taken into account. There are situations where two pawns are stronger than a queen, others where one side has a forced win even though he is three pieces down. *If we are about to give checkmate, it doesn't matter how many extra pieces the opponent has.* Everything depends on the exact position on the board. In fact it is here, in a growing understanding and intuition of the subtleties of judging 'the whole picture', that a chess-player's natural talent for the game *and* the progress he makes become most clearly visible.

Nevertheless, there are guidelines for evaluating the pieces, as there are guidelines for everything, and it is important to know them, since they apply much more often than not. So here we go:

The value of the king is undefined since it cannot be captured, let alone traded for another piece. All other pieces are valued in points: a queen is usually given 9 points, a rook 5, bishop and knight both get 3 points and a pawn is worth 1 point.

Queen	9
Rook	5
Bishop	3
Knight	3
Pawn	1

You should memorize this table.

This means that a bishop and knight are of roughly equal value and that both are worth three pawns. A rook is worth more than a bishop or a knight separately, but it will struggle against the two of them combined. A queen is worth three minor pieces, but two rooks are (or rather they *can* be) a little stronger.

As you become more experienced as a player, you will develop a more nuanced feel for when certain pieces can become worth more or less than this table suggests, and which pairings of pieces tend to perform best.

The Basic Mates

Another important consideration for comparing the value of the pieces is that a queen will always be able to checkmate a lone king, as will a rook, but neither bishop nor knight is powerful enough to accomplish this.

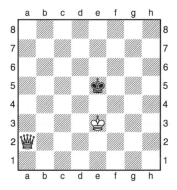

The checkmating process can be divided into two different phases. First the black king needs to be driven to one of the four edges of the board, since with so little material left there is no way to checkmate the king anywhere else. This the queen can do alone, though the process is both speeded up and made easier if the king also lends a hand. In the second phase, the actual checkmating itself, the king *has* to take part. So here we have, for the first time in this book, a situation where the king is not a liability in constant need of protection, but a fighting unit. Of course he can only safely do this because a lone king can never pose any sort of threat to his opposite number: it is illegal for the kings even to stand on squares that are next to each other, as they would both be in check.

The whole process is actually pretty straightforward, but right at the end White usually has to avoid one last trap: stalemate.

1 ♕a5+

There are many other moves that are equally good. The variation given here is only an example.

1...♚e6 2 ♚e4

King and queen are working together well. Both of them are taking away squares from the black king, who is quickly driven to the edge of the board.

2...♚d6 3 ♕b6+ ♚e7 4 ♚e5 ♚f7

In case of 4...♚d7 5 ♕b7+ ♚e8 6 ♚e6 things go a little faster.

5 ♚f5 ♚e7 6 ♕c7+ ♚f8 7 ♚f6

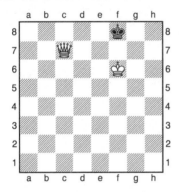

Position after 7 ♚f6
Black to move

Mate on the next move is now unavoidable. If Black plays 7...♚g8 it is 8 ♕g7# that does the trick and if 7...♚e8 White even has two moves that give checkmate: 8 ♕c8# and 8 ♕e7#. But White must be careful here not to *stalemate* the black king: after 7...♚e8 both 8 ♕d6?? and 8 ♚g7?? would be stalemate and thus a draw.

The reader will have noticed that mate and stalemate are sometimes perilously close to each other in this type of endgame, especially once the enemy king has been pushed to the edge of the board. What makes this endgame so treacherous is that it is *necessary* for the enemy king to be robbed of its freedom of movement. It is only at the very end of the chase that the risk of stalemating (instead of checkmating) arises. Thousands of players have relaxed one move too soon in this type of endgame and seen their quarry escape at the last possible moment.

Let us, for instance, go back to the position after 1 ♕a5+ and suppose that Black, instead of going backwards (1...♚e6), decides to withdraw his king to the h-file.

1 ♕a5+ ♚f6 2 ♚f4 ♚g6 3 ♕b6+ ♚h5

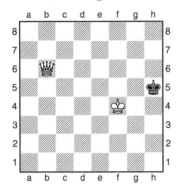

Position after 3...♚h5
White to move

The black king has walked into a mating-net, but it is not mate just yet. What could be more natural than to pull the net a little tighter still?

4 ♕f6??

"Surely this is going to be mate on the very next move." Unfortunately for White, there won't be a next move. It is stalemate and the game is over.

The irony in this way of thinking is that every other queen move along the sixth rank (with the obvious exceptions of 4 ♕g6+?? and 4 ♕h6+??) would have done the trick. After 4 ♕a6, for example, Black has only one move and that will be his last: 4...♚h4 5 ♕h6#.

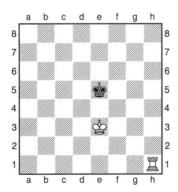

With a rook instead of a queen, the overall winning method remains basically the same: first the black king is pushed to the edge of the board, and then he is mated. Since a rook is less powerful than a queen, this takes a little more time and the help of the king is needed both in the first and in the second phase, but otherwise there are no great difficulties. And the great thing about a rook not being as powerful as a queen is that there is little risk of an accidental stalemate!

1 ♖h5+

Again, White has a good many moves to realize his plan. There is no hurry. Once the general idea is understood, the moves come automatically. First the black king is pushed to the edge of the board.

1...♚d6 2 ♚e4

By playing this move rather than 2 ♚d4, which if you are planning to shoulder the black king backwards is perhaps the more obvious move, White is anticipating that the black king will try to stay in the centre by replying 2...♚e6. This would now allow White to push the king one rank closer to the back rank with 3 ♖h6+, which would not have been the case had White played 2 ♚d4 for then 2...♚e6 3 ♖h6+ could have been answered by 3...♚f5.

2...♚c6 3 ♚d4

Same plan again! If now 3...♚d6, White will play 4 ♖h6+ and the black king is pushed back to the seventh rank.

3...♚b6

But now of course Black is getting dangerously close to being cut off on the a-file.

4 ♚c4 ♚c6

And that's why he now tries to return to the centre. If 4...♚a6 5 ♖b5, phase one would have been accomplished.

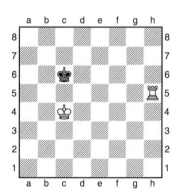

Position after 4...♚c6
White to move

Now White can of course play 5 ♖h6+, followed by a king move to c5 or d5, a repetition of the technique he has been using up to this point. But there is another method of incarcerating the enemy king that works equally well.

5 ♖d5

No check, yet highly effective. The black king is now condemned to the area (or should I say cage?) a8-a6-c6-c8. His fate is sealed.

5...♚c7 6 ♚b5 ♚b7 7 ♖d7+ ♚c8 8 ♚c6 ♚b8

Black's king has almost no room left, and this is the only move. It is clear that we have reached the final episode, in which White has to find a checkmate. For this we will use a subtle weapon, which is of colossal importance in endgame technique throughout (indeed we already made use of it when checkmating with the queen): *zugzwang*.

9 ♖d8+ ♚a7 10 ♖h8

In fact (almost) any rook move along the eighth rank suffices, for Black now *has* to play the one move he is desperate to avoid: 10...♚a6, allowing 11 ♖a8#.

We call this *zugzwang* (German for "compulsion to move") because there is actually no threat, so if it were possible to 'pass' (i.e. choose not to make a move at all) Black wouldn't have a problem. However, the rules of chess don't allow this: when it is our turn to move, we *must* make a move. Black is forced to worsen his position, and fatally so.

Just to remind ourselves: we 'narrowly' avoided one of the very few possible stalemates in this type of ending by not playing 9 ♖b7+ (instead of 9 ♖d8+) 9...♚a8 10 ♚b6?? stalemate (or 10 ♚c7?? stalemate).

It becomes clear then that checkmating a lone king with king and rook is not terribly difficult. Even if White does not play with any great accuracy he will usually manage to win well before the fifty-move rule (see page 25) comes into play.

> *Chess study:* Make sure you keep a copy of your scoresheet of each game you play (or save a copy on your computer if you have played online). Study these games later, assessing what you did right and what went wrong. Be objective. Once you have done so, check your conclusions with a computer and share them with a chess-playing friend.

The term 'endgame' is used when there are few pieces left on the board. It does not necessarily imply that the end is near. On the contrary, endgames often last a very long time. It is not a coincidence that the fifty-move rule almost exclusively comes into effect in endgames.

When we discuss a game of chess we normally distinguish between the 'opening' (a term we have already used in Lesson 4), the 'middlegame' and the 'endgame' (if there is one – a lot of games do not go beyond the middlegame). The lines between opening and middlegame or between middlegame and endgame are not very clearly defined. Some people start talking about an 'endgame' not long after the queens have been exchanged, while others reserve the term for positions like the above where there are very few pieces left.

With bishop and king against king there is no way to give checkmate – and indeed under the rules of chess this ending is a *draw by insufficient material*.

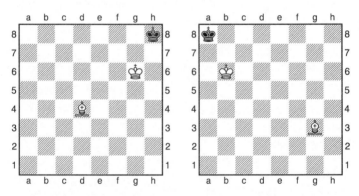

The maximum possible White can achieve is trapping the enemy king in a corner. In the left-hand position, it is check, but not mate. Black plays 1...♚g8 and nothing happens. After 2 ♗g7 it is stalemate.

In the right-hand diagram, White again simply has not enough firepower. If it is Black to move it is stalemate.

The same goes for a knight – king and knight vs king is also a draw by insufficient material.

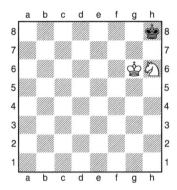

White has made all the progress that he could hope for: the black king is immobilized on a corner square. Yet stalemate is all he could ever possibly achieve. There simply is no way for king and knight to cover all the necessary squares for a checkmate (h8, g8, h7 and g7).

All endgames that we have looked at in this lesson are called 'elementary' endgames, partly because there are so few pieces left on the board but mainly because of their overwhelming importance. They underlie all of the more complex endgames. Anyone starting to play chess will quickly realize their importance once they actually have to find a mate with king and queen against a lone king for the first time.

Can You Mate with Just Two Minor Pieces?

We will take our examination of the elementary endgames just a little bit further. While a single bishop is not enough to checkmate a lone king, *two bishops* combined (i.e. king and two bishops vs king) will do the trick. Again the general idea is first to trap the enemy king in one of the corners, and then to checkmate him. The procedure is not too complicated, though you need to coordinate the two bishops and the king to confine and drive back the enemy king. It is worth practising it with a friend or against a computer.

Strangely enough (and a good illustration of how relative any system of valuing the pieces really is), the ending with *two knights* instead of two bishops is a totally different affair. According to our table, two knights should be equally powerful as two bishops, but the reality is that they cannot force checkmate against a lone king. But note that this ending is *not* a draw by insufficient material, as it is possible for a mate to occur, though it would require a major blunder by the defender for this to happen. If his king is cornered, he merely needs to choose the right square for this king to avoid a snap mate.

With *knight plus bishop* things are different yet again! Theoretically this is a forced win, but in practice one has to play really, really well in order to win it. In fact the winning procedure is much more complicated than any of the other 'basic mates' and an examination of this endgame would fall well outside the scope of this book. It is just worth noting that in order to force mate, the enemy king must be driven into one of the two corners where the bishop can control the corner square itself – mate cannot be forced in the other two corners.

Chess preparation: Once you have started playing serious chess, you'll want to learn something about openings. At least have a plan for what you will play as White (generally 1 e4 or 1 d4) and how you will answer those two moves as Black. Consider getting a one-volume opening guide to help you choose openings that you like.

Our exercises for this lesson feature these three endgames.

There remains one more term related to the value of the pieces which we have not mentioned yet: *the exchange*. This term is used to denote the difference in value between a rook on one side and a minor piece (a bishop or a knight) on the other.

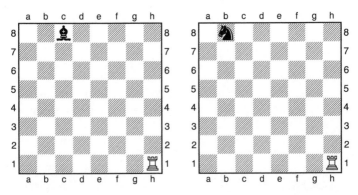

In both these diagrams White is *the exchange up*, and Black is *the exchange down*.

Exercises

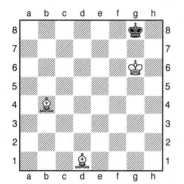

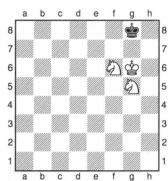

11) This is the final stage of mating with two bishops. White has a 'mate in two', i.e. he can force checkmate in two moves. Both moves have to be accurate. White moves first and then has a checkmate on his next move after any reply by Black. Can you find it?

12) This diagram shows the critical position if a player fruitlessly tries to mate with just two knights. Black's king is in check, and he has two possible escape-squares. Which way should he go?

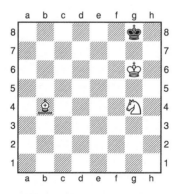

13) The final stage of mating with bishop and knight, once the king is trapped in the 'correct' corner, is not so difficult. In this position White has a mate in two moves. Can you find it?

Lesson 6: An Aggressive Opening

Let us now return to the initial position.

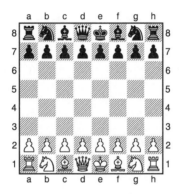

Once you start playing chess, one thing is certain: this position will come back in every single game that you will ever play. So it is worthwhile thinking about it a little. But you won't be the first to do so. Thinking about how to open a game and sharing these thoughts with others is what millions of chess-players have done for centuries. This has resulted in a huge body of what we call 'opening theory'. Putting it like this makes it sound rather theoretical, but in reality opening theory is nothing but tried and tested practice. Now what exactly does opening theory look like and what use is it to someone who has only just started learning the game?

Most libraries are not big enough to contain all the chess books dealing with opening theory alone. Novice chess-players may find it hard to imagine that most opening books are out of date within a few years of publication so that room (and demand) for new books on the same subject is created continually and automatically. Because many opening manuals deal with just one opening (or even just one variation of a particular opening), the total production in this segment of the chess book market is huge.

However, this does not mean that a novice is faced with a hopeless task here. Anyone who wants to learn about openings has a choice of more learner-oriented manuals which tend to explain existing variations rather than try to find new ones and consequently do not become obsolete quite so quickly. Besides, there is no real need for studying opening theory at all while you are still learning the basics. *If* you should turn out to be really interested in this particular aspect of the game you will come across a good learner's guide soon enough and probably at a stage where you already have some experience and are better able to decide what it is exactly that you want from an opening book.

To start with, it is more than enough to learn some of the terminology, the guiding principles and the general ideas about what to do and what not to do. Let us therefore just start another game and see what happens.

1 e4

If there is *one* guiding principle on how to play the opening, it has to be "develop your pieces". Get them out! Get them into play! It is like the first thing you need to know about learning how to drive a car: get it out of the garage.

This might lead one to think of 1 ♘f3 or any other of the four possible knight moves as the best way to start a game, and there is certainly nothing wrong with that. But the knights can't go it alone and in order to make room for the other pieces some of the pawns will have to move. This brings us to another very important principle: "the pawns are the soul of chess", a lesson first taught by André Philidor, the greatest chess-player *and* theoretician of the 18th century. As we are about to see, the character of almost any position is largely defined by what is called its *pawn-structure*. Anyone learning the game will at first only be able to see separate pawns and pieces on the board, but on becoming more adept he will start to see the whole board with all the pieces on it as one living organism. Of this organism the pawns form the skeleton. Only rarely will any of the pieces venture out 'on their own'. In almost every situation they will adapt their movements to whatever the pawn-structure requires of them. We have already seen an example of this in Lesson 4, where White succumbed due to a serious weakening of his pawn-structure on the kingside.

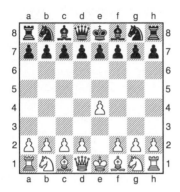

Position after 1 e4
Black to move

1...e5

There are twenty possible replies to 1 e4, yet in practice only about half of them are frequently used, the rest of them being almost non-existent as far as opening theory is concerned. We have already seen that 1...d5 is an aggressive option and that this opening is called the Scandinavian Defence. Other popular defences to 1 e4 are: 1...c5, the Sicilian Defence (which is the most popular chess opening of all); 1...e6, the French Defence; 1...c6, the Caro-Kann; 1...d6, the Pirc Defence; 1...♘f6, the Alekhine Defence; and 1...g6, the Modern Defence. Most of Black's other options are thought to contribute too little to a rapid and effective piece development, though some of them (most notably 1...♘c6 and 1...b6) aren't bad at all. Examples of bad moves are 1...b5?, which loses a pawn outright to 2 ♗xb5, as does 1...f5? after 2 exf5. 1...a5? doesn't lose material, but fails to get any pieces into play and ignores the all-important *central* squares (d4, d5, e4 and e5).

By playing 1...e5 Black copies his opponent's strategy – a *symmetrical* reply. There is no name for 1...e5, perhaps because this move used to be Black's almost self-evident choice for such a long time (until about the middle of the 19th century) that naming it was not thought necessary.

It is perhaps as well to inform the reader that there is very little logic in chess opening nomenclature and that an opening may carry different names in different language areas. In this book, however, we will only deal with some of the most frequently used openings whose names are almost universally accepted.

2 ♘f3

Now White develops a knight. He does so in a rather aggressive way since the knight is threatening the e5-pawn. Other moves that have been given the seal of approval over the centuries are: 2 ♘c3, the Vienna Game; 2 ♗c4, the Bishop's Opening; 2 f4, the King's Gambit; and 2 d4, the Centre Game. The term 'gambit' is used for an opening (or a variation of an opening) where one side is prepared to make a material sacrifice (usually a pawn) in order to speed up his development, open an important file or achieve some other positional advantage. In the King's Gambit, for example, by playing 2 f4 White hopes in the long term to profit from the absence of a black pawn on e5 (after 2...exf4) by building a strong and flexible *pawn-centre* with a later d4 pawn advance (usually 3 ♘f3 is played first in order to prevent 3...♕h4+). It is a risky strategy, though not necessarily a bad one.

Naturally, all this is rather advanced strategic thinking and not something to worry about in the context of this book. With respect to material, every novice's first guideline should be to *capture* any material that is free for the taking rather than to give it away. Sacrificing comes later.

We now return to 2 ♘f3:

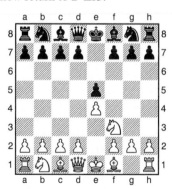

Position after 2 ♘f3
Black to move

2...♘c6

Black too develops a knight in a purposeful manner. The pawn on e5 is now protected. Two important alternatives are 2...d6, the Philidor Defence, and 2...♘f6, the Petroff Defence. The latter defence is actually a counterattack, because instead of worrying about his pawn on e5 Black threatens e4.

3 d4

With this move the opening is finally given its name: the Scotch Opening. Major alternatives are: 3 ♗b5, the Ruy Lopez (the most popular); 3 ♗c4, the Italian Game; and 3 ♘c3 which (after 3...♘f6) is called the Four Knights Game. Incidentally, one should realize that many of these openings are interconnected. For instance, the position after 3 ♗b5 ♘f6 4 ♘c3 is identical to the one after 3 ♘c3 ♘f6 4 ♗b5. When studying one particular opening, *transpositions* like these always have to be kept in mind.

By playing 3 d4 White makes room for his queen and bishop, while at the same time attacking e5. This is a straightforward opening strategy, with White opening hostilities at the first opportunity. A somewhat slower strategy would involve moves like 3 ♗c4 ♗c5 (this is called the Giuoco Piano) 4 d3. Here White is not in a hurry to attack the e5-pawn and is more likely to keep playing useful developing moves (like ♘c3, ♗e3 and 0-0) for a while before starting any sort of attack.

A third way of tackling the 'opening problem' is to prepare the d4 advance by playing c3 first. White intends to recapture on d4 with his c-pawn should Black decide to play ...exd4. This would give him a strong central position with pawns on e4 and d4.

Which of these options is best is impossible to say. They are all intrinsically

> *Chess study:* If your chess club (or favourite online site) features lectures, attend some of them. Be bold and ask questions!

sound, but they all lead to different pawn-structures and each player should choose the type of position which suits his temperament and his abilities best. On average the aggressive player/personality would perhaps be inclined to play 3 d4, while a more careful one might prefer one of the other two options, while an original thinker might come up with a fourth. But one thing is made very clear at this juncture: it is the pawn moves that determine our long-term decisions. We call these *strategic* decisions as opposed to *tactical* decisions. 'Tactics' refers to solving concrete issues, and mainly requires imagination and accuracy in short-term thinking, also known as calculation. Just as in 'real life', most players have a natural inclination towards one or the other of these fundamental aspects of chess, although skill in both is required to play successfully. Anyone learning the game should study both tactics and strategy.

We now return to 3 d4:

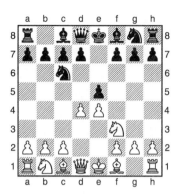

Position after 3 d4
Black to move

3...exd4

Black decides to give up his stronghold on e5 now that a good opportunity presents itself to *exchange* the pawn. The term 'exchanging' is used for trading a piece (or a pawn) for a piece (or pieces) of the same value, for instance a bishop for a knight, a rook for a knight and two pawns, or a pawn for a pawn.

4 ♘xd4

White recaptures the pawn. Even though the game has barely started, the tension between the opposing armies is quickly becoming palpable. Black is already in a position to capture a knight (4...♘xd4), though this does not lead to any material gain because White would simply recapture (5 ♕xd4), thus maintaining the balance. The two most important *variations* of the Scotch are 4...♗c5 and 4...♘f6. Both moves are aggressive in that they develop a piece while introducing a threat at the same time: 4...♗c5 attacks the knight on d4, while 4...♘f6 attacks e4.

> *Tactics training:* It's really important to practise solving tactical positions. There are some good books to choose from, both to learn important tactical patterns and to practise finding ways to use them to win games.

The term 'variation' – or 'line' – is used for a series of moves within a particular opening, often with a name of its own; e.g., the 'Najdorf Variation of the Sicilian Defence', named after the famous grandmaster Miguel Najdorf.

4...♘f6

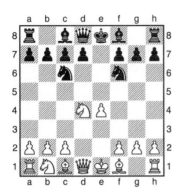

Position after 4...♘f6
White to move

Playing aggressive moves in the opening usually not only creates opportunities but also involves taking certain risks and all too often the pros and cons of such moves are difficult to evaluate. In playing 4...♘f6 Black is taking the 'risk' that White now chases the knight away from f6 by lashing out with 5 ♘xc6 bxc6 6 e5. This is in fact an important (and rather aggressive) opening variation, but for this instructive game I think we should prefer something a little more conservative.

5 ♘c3

A useful developing move. The e4-pawn is now protected.

5...♗b4

By now something of what is meant by 'develop your pieces quickly and aggressively' should come across. Again Black brings a piece into play while attacking an enemy piece: the knight on c3 is now *pinned* so that the pawn on e4 once again finds itself under attack.

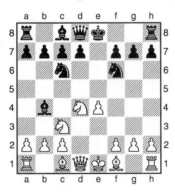

Position after 5...♗b4
White to move

6 ♘xc6

White cannot play the developing move 6 ♗d3?? to protect e4 for this would cost him a knight: 6...♘xd4. He therefore exchanges knights first.

6...bxc6

Restoring the material balance. Black now has doubled pawns, but because they are still connected to another pawn, his d-pawn, this does not result in a major weakening of his pawn-structure (as it did in Lesson 4). The pawns provide each other with support. Also Black now has the option of making an advance in the centre that he did not have before the exchange on c6: he can play ...d5, when a possible exd5 can now be met by ...cxd5. (Remember that three dots implies a move by Black; these moves are given without move-numbers because they are general ideas in the position that could occur at some point.)

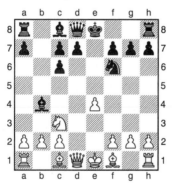

Position after 6...bxc6
White to move

7 ♗d3

Now that the knights have been exchanged, this useful developing move can be safely played.

7...d5

Again Black is threatening the e4-pawn. These repeated attacks against e4 might lead one to suspect that this pawn has advanced too far and constitutes a weakness in White's position, but it is actually the other way round. It is precisely *because* the pawn is so well placed on e4 that Black keeps battering it, hoping to remove this stronghold.

8 exd5

And here we could say that the pawn has done its job. It has taken an active and important part in the opening battle and it can now safely say goodbye.

8...cxd5

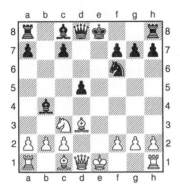

Position after 8...cxd5
White to move

9 0-0 0-0

With the e-file now open, it was high time for the kings to get out of the way and seek refuge on the kingside. At the same time, castling is also a way of developing the rooks. Whereas they took little or no part in the game while still on their original squares (h1 and h8), on f1 and f8 they are ready for active duty.

10 ♗g5

White's last remaining minor piece joins the battle. This is often the way a game develops: first some of the pawns make a move, then the minor pieces and only then do the major pieces join in. I am not sure whether we should call this a guideline, because the order in which the pieces make their first moves *always* depends on the exact circumstances, but on the other hand the statistics strongly suggest that it *is* a guideline. Let's keep it at that.

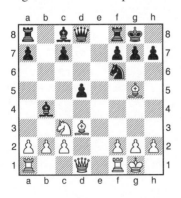

Position after 10 ♗g5
Black to move

By putting his bishop on g5, White has introduced a veiled threat into the position: 11 ♗xf6. Now recapturing with the queen would leave d5 unprotected (11...♕xf6 12 ♘xd5) but even 11...gxf6 is not safe, for White can still play 12 ♘xd5!. If Black recaptures by 12...♕xd5? he loses the queen to the surprising 13 ♗xh7+! ♔xh7 14 ♕xd5.

This is in fact a standard *combination*. At first glance the queen appears safe on d5 but because the bishop on d3 vacates the d-file *with check* (which means that Black *has* to do something about it) this turns out not to be the case.

The term 'combination' is used for a sequence of two or more moves by which a concrete, tactical success is achieved, usually with an element of surprise to it. A combination normally involves a *sacrifice* of material.

The crucial move in this combination, 12 ♘xd5, may be termed a 'sacrifice', for with this move White gives away a knight. However, the investment pays dividends very quickly, and such moves are sometimes called 'sham sacrifices', to distinguish them from true sacrifices, which involve a greater degree of risk and uncertainty.

However, it is Black to move, and he has a chance of parry White's threat.

10...♗e6

There are other ways to ward off the threat of 11 ♗xf6 (like 10...c6 or 10...♗xc3), but in this game both players make a point of developing their pieces as quickly as possible.

11 ♕f3

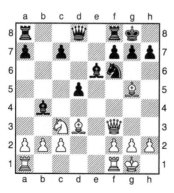

Position after 11 ♕f3
Black to move

Another developing move and again it comes with a threat, though this time of a positional nature: 12 ♗xf6, which would saddle Black with doubled (and isolated!) f-pawns. Still, this is a difficult strategic decision to make: is this really advantageous for White? It might be worthwhile to look more deeply at a move like 11...♖b8 (*activating* the rook, for it now controls the b-file), allowing the exchange 12 ♗xf6 ♕xf6 13 ♕xf6 gxf6 on the grounds that the doubled pawns are only nominally weak while Black has plenty of *compensation* in the form of free piece-play. But this is a problem for the more advanced player to solve. For us it is sufficient to take note of the fact that such questions exist.

11...♗e7

Black does not 'risk' it. He provides the knight with some additional protection and in so doing also *breaks the pin*. Whether this is the best move or not, when I reveal who these two players were, it will become obvious that Black did indeed know what he was doing.

12 ♖fe1

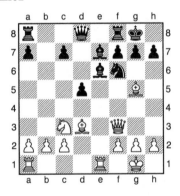

Position after 12 ♖fe1
Black to move

A rook always feels best on what is called an *open file* – a file where there are no pawns left. The greater its freedom of movement, the more powerful it becomes.

12...h6

Black has several other good moves in this position, for instance 12...♖b8 or 12...♖e8. But Black decides to take the bull by the horns.

The bishop on g5 is now attacked. Where will it go?

13 ♗xh6!

Now *this* is a sacrifice! And there is more to come...

The exclamation mark is for courage and for accuracy in calculating variations, not for the objective value of this move. White might equally well have retreated the bishop, for instance to f4.

13...gxh6

Black is a piece up. How should White continue?

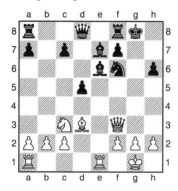

Position after 13...gxh6
White to move

14 ♖xe6!

Another sacrifice, this time of the exchange.

14...fxe6

And still it is not clear what the point of White's combination is.

15 ♕g3+

Black has two possible king moves to get out of the check, but on closer examination only one of them is really playable for 15...♔f7?? runs into 16 ♕g6#!.

15...♔h8

This looks like a safe haven for the king. There is no mate. Now how does White justify his sacrifices (which by now total a whole rook)?

16 ♕g6!

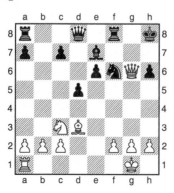

Position after 16 ♕g6!
Black to move

The point of White's combination and a fine example of how un-fathomably deep really strong players are sometimes able to look ahead.

White is threatening to continue 17 ♕xh6+, which will give him a draw by repetition at least (17...♔g8 18 ♕g6+ or 18 ♕g5+, etc.). Should Black for instance play 16...♗d6 (in order to make room for the queen to join the defence via e7 and g7) White would simply play 17 ♕xh6+ ♔g8 18 ♕g6+ ♔h8 19 ♕h6+, when Black cannot avoid a repetition of moves. If 16...♕e8 instead, White achieves the same result with 17 ♕xh6+ ♔g8 18 ♕g5+ ♔h8 19 ♕h6+, etc. The black king has no way out of the checks.

This specific form of draw by repetition, with one side giving check and his opponent unable to escape the checks, is called a *perpetual check*. The term 'perpetual' should not of course be taken literally since when a position arises for the third time White (or Black) will simply claim a draw (see Lesson 2) and the game is over.

> *Social media:* There is plenty of chess content and news on sites such as Facebook and Twitter. Many major chess events have Twitter feeds, and you'll doubtless find some chess Tweeters whom you'll want to follow. Many of the top players – including the World Champion – are often found on Twitter.

There is no way Black can avoid the perpetual check. If 16...♖g8??, 17 ♕xh6+ leads to mate on the next move (17...♘h7 18 ♕xh7#) while 16...♘g8?? even allows a mate in one: 17 ♕h7#. In our game Black therefore accepted the draw that was offered to him by his opponent when he played 16 ♕g6.

This was a game from 1914 between two of the greatest players of all time. Playing Black was the then world champion Emanuel Lasker, while his opponent was Alexander Alekhine, destined to become world champion himself thirteen years later.

The finale of this game is a good example of a combination. First White sacrifices a piece, then an exchange and by doing so he is able to achieve a draw by repetition, a result he was obviously happy with in this game. Let us consider this combination again from the beginning.

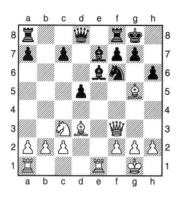

Position after 12...h6
White to move

In order to be successful, a combination must always to a certain extent force the opponent's reply. This is clearly the case here. After 13 ♗xh6 Black *has* to capture the bishop for otherwise he would just lose a pawn for nothing. So 13...gxh6 is 'forced' (to a certain extent that is – being a pawn down is not necessarily the end of the world). Then 14 ♖xe6 has the same effect: Black *has* to reply 14...fxe6 if he does not want to be a pawn down for nothing. But after White's next move, 15 ♕g3+, there is one move that we have not considered yet: 15...♘g4. Black returns a whole piece in order to disrupt White's attacking scheme, for after 16 ♕xg4+ he can now use his bishop to block the check: 16...♗g5, a resource that was not available to him with the knight still on f6. Even so, White's combination is fully correct. White continues with 17 ♕xe6+ ♔h8 18 ♘xd5 (18 ♕g6 would now be met by 18...♕d7, covering the h7-square and thus preventing 19 ♕h7#), reaching the following position.

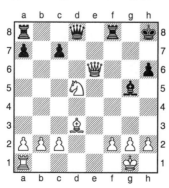

Position after 18 ♘xd5
Black to move

Black has managed to defend against the mating threats, but with three pawns for the exchange (Black is a rook 'up' but a knight and three pawns 'down') the resulting material balance is in White's favour. It goes without saying that there is a lot of life left and that anything is still possible in this position, but this analysis clearly confirms that 15...♘g4 is (to say the least) not better objectively than 15...♔h8, which resulted in a quick draw.

With the above discussion of Alekhine's combination we have left what can be called the opening behind us and have almost imperceptibly entered a new phase: the middlegame. This is not a coincidence. A game of chess is conventionally divided into opening, middlegame and endgame, but to draw distinct boundaries between these three stages is virtually impossible.

Exercises

In this lesson we have learned a great deal about *combinations*. They can be divided into different types yet they often have one or more standard elements in common. Knowing these can be very useful. Let us start practising a little.

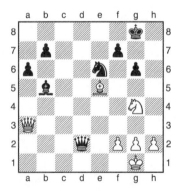

14) White to move. Black is a pawn up and at first glance there seems to be nothing wrong with his position. But if we look a little deeper it turns out that White can win Black's queen within three moves by force. How?

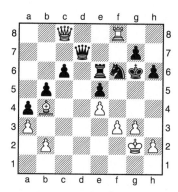

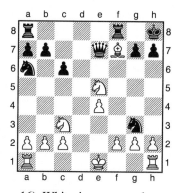

15) Again it is White to move, again Black's position *appears* solid and again there is a way for White to win a queen. Can you find it?

16) White is a queen down. His position looks hopeless. And yet he has a mate by force in just three moves! Can you spot it? Remember this: rooks love open files, but kings hate them!

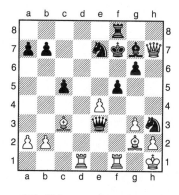

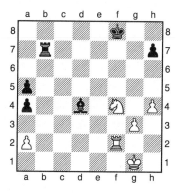

17) Things are looking rather gloomy for Black. He is already an exchange down and White is threatening to take another piece, either on g7 or on h3. But Black has a truly fantastic move in this position, a real killer blow. It's checkmate in two moves; can you find it?

18) White's rook is pinned and it looks like the loss of the exchange is unavoidable, yet there is one move for White that turns the tables. Not only does it save the rook, but it even wins the black bishop! Which move is this?

Lesson 7: A Cautious Opening

Let us return once more to the initial position. In the previous lesson we have seen how rapidly hostilities can break out if both sides play aggressively right from the start. But this is not the only possible way of handling the opening. For those who prefer a more cautious approach there are openings where the battle tends to unfold at a somewhat slower pace. Generally speaking, these openings are of a more strategic nature with positional considerations taking centre stage, while in openings like the Scotch (as in the previous lesson) it is mainly tactics (threats, combinations and sacrifices) that need to be foremost in the players' minds. However, it is important to remember that strategy and tactics are really two sides of the same coin. They cannot exist without each other. Even when your thinking is mostly strategic, tactics are never far away.

1 d4

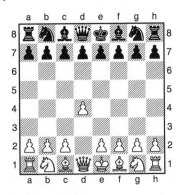

Position after 1 d4
Black to move

This opening move is often preferred by positionally oriented players, i.e. those who are naturally inclined to think strategically rather than tactically. The difference from 1 e4 lies mainly in the position of the pawn on d4, which is protected by the queen on d1 and therefore less exposed to an immediate attack than White's e-pawn is after 1 e4. This may sound like a recommendation of 1 d4, but in reality the difference between 1 e4 and 1 d4 is very much a matter of taste. In fact, even claiming that 1 d4 is the positional player's move and 1 e4 the tactician's choice is rather an exaggeration. A fierce and highly tactical battle may result from 1 d4 just as easily as 1 e4 may lead to a slow, positional game. It is not the first move that decides the course of the game, but the whole of the players' preferences and the specific interaction between them.

1...♘f6

The symmetrical reply 1...d5 has similar merits to White's own first move. For while White's pawn on d4 is indeed firmly protected, so is its counterpart on d5. This has direct consequences for White's second move, for in this position 2 ♘c3 (unlike the analogous opening 1 e4 e5 2 ♘f3) does *not* attack a pawn so while this is still a reasonable developing move, it puts little immediate pressure on Black's position, and is rarely played.

On the other hand, 1 d4 d5 allows White to play the aggressive 2 c4.

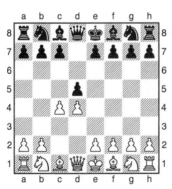

Position after 2 c4
Black to move

We saw briefly in the previous lesson that the analogous 1 e4 e5 2 f4 is a double-edged gambit, to say the least. But after 1 d4 d5 2 c4, if Black takes the proffered pawn on c4 (2...dxc4) White can regain the pawn rather easily, so this opening – called the Queen's Gambit – is far less risky, and much more popular. Depending on Black's reply this is further divided into the Queen's Gambit Declined (2...e6), the Slav Defence (2...c6) and the Queen's Gambit Accepted (2...dxc4).

1...d5, 1...♘f6 and 1...f5 (the Dutch Defence) are all intended to stop White from dominating the centre by playing 2 e4. Black may also decide to allow this move and postpone open warfare until his development has been completed. This is a strategic decision, comparable to White's decision to try to take immediate control of the centre (1 e4 or 1 d4) or not (e.g. 1 g3 or 1 b3). Opening theory is always mainly concerned with aggressive openings, so these are the ones that can be (and *have* to be) studied in greater detail.

Incidentally, it may be worth our while to take a somewhat closer look at the Dutch Defence, since this opening nicely illustrates the possibility of developing pieces *without* making contact with the enemy at the first opportunity. One of the main lines of the Leningrad Variation of the Dutch goes like this: 1 d4 f5 2 g3 ♘f6 3 ♗g2 g6 4 ♘f3 ♗g7 5 0-0 0-0 6 c4 d6 7 ♘c3 ♕e8.

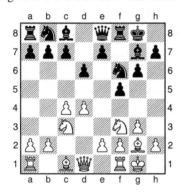

Position after 7...♕e8
White to move

Seven moves have been played without any direct contact between the two armies. Black's last move is a preparation for the central thrust 8...e5 which means that hostilities are (finally!) likely to break out.

This then is a way of playing the opening without any immediate necessity of drawing your gun or running for cover. There are many openings like this, especially in the 1 d4 range. Choosing between an opening of this or the 'aggressive' type is to a very large extent a matter of taste. In chess (as in life) there is often no 'best move' but a whole range of possibilities of more or less equal value.

Let's return to 1...♘f6.

2 c4

By pushing a second pawn forward, White increases his influence over the centre.

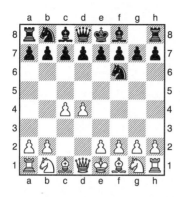

Position after 2 c4
Black to move

There are some good alternatives (e.g. 2 ♘f3 and 2 ♘c3, both solid developing moves), but 2 c4 is regarded by opening theory as the most ambitious move. For this reason we will take it as our main line here. Even when you are not interested in *following* opening theory (as a player) it is still worthwhile to *know* about it (as a student). Getting an inkling of how opening theory works and why it selects the moves it does select is the best way of getting to a level where you can make your own decisions in the opening and perhaps create your own repertoire of openings.

2...g6

Black prepares to develop his dark-squared bishop to g7. From there it will command the long a1-h8 diagonal and be well-placed to exert considerable pressure on the centre and on White's queenside. The technical term for developing a bishop to g7 or b7 (or g2 or b2 for White) is a *fianchetto*. The bishop is 'fianchettoed'. The word was taken from the Italian (it means 'little flank') in a time when that language was dominant in chess literature: the 17th century.

Another important set of openings begins with 2...e6. If then 3 ♘c3 ♝b4 we have a Nimzo-Indian Defence while 3 ♘f3 b6 is called the Queen's Indian Defence. Black keeps his pawn-structure flexible as long as possible. He stops White from playing e4, but refuses to commit himself in any other way.

Another popular opening is 2...c5, the Benoni Defence. Black is not worried about 3 dxc5 because 3...e6 followed by ...♝xc5 would regain the pawn at once. White's most ambitious (and theoretically interesting) reply is in fact 3 d5.

We now return to 2...g6:

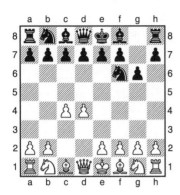

Position after 2...g6
White to move

3 ♘c3

In this type of position c3 is the perfect square for the queen's knight: it controls two central squares, e4 and d5. There are other developing moves (e.g. 3 ♘f3 or 3 g3 followed by 4 ♗g2), but 3 ♘c3 is the most ambitious.

3...♗g7

By playing this move, the natural follow up to 2...g6, Black puts his cards on the table: he is not going to challenge White's supremacy in the centre just yet. This is the King's Indian Defence. Its twin brother, though with an entirely different character, is 3...d5, the Grünfeld Defence. This move does not really do anything to stop White from playing e4 either, but the difference is that Black immediately opens the d-file (and – in many cases – the a1-h8 diagonal) in order to start a counterattack against d4. One of the crucial variations is 4 cxd5 ♘xd5 5 e4 ♘xc3 6 bxc3 ♗g7 followed by 7...c5.

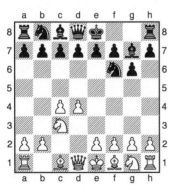

Position after 3...♗g7
White to move

4 e4

Accepting the challenge. There is no obligation to do this. Developing moves like 4 ♘f3, 4 ♗g5 or 4 g3 are perfectly alright, but again opening theory is primarily interested in the most ambitious, the most energetic moves, so 4 e4 has become the main line.

With 4 e4 we have reached what may be termed the starting position of the King's Indian Defence. There are a huge number of variations and subvariations to this opening, a discussion of which falls outside the scope of this book. But I would like to draw your attention to a typical pawn-formation which may arise from many of these subvariations and which nicely illustrates (again) how it is almost always the pawn-structure that determines the course of the game. The next five moves are given without commentary (though note that there are alternatives for both sides throughout this sequence).

4...d6 5 ♘f3 0-0 6 ♗e2 e5 7 0-0 ♘c6 8 d5 ♘e7

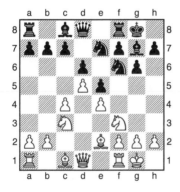

Position after 8...♘e7
White to move

The difference between this game and the ones from Lessons 4 and 6 is twofold: all the central pawns are still on the board *and* they have all come to a complete halt to form what is called a 'closed' position. Both sides will now have to play 'around' the central wall that has been formed. For White this means that he will follow a strategy based on playing either c5 or f4 to attack Black's side of the wall and for Black that he is likely to do the same with ...f5 or ...c6 (or both). It is clear that a game like this normally takes a long time to heat up, but I can tell you that once both sides' plans reach their climax the heat may well become unbearable (while Open Games often tend to fizzle out quickly, as we saw in Lesson 6, the Alekhine-Lasker game). Let us suppose, for example, that the game continues like this:

9 ♘e1 ♘d7 10 ♘d3 f5 11 ♗d2 ♘f6 12 f3 f4 13 c5 g5 14 ♖c1 ♘g6 15 ♘b5 ♖f7 16 cxd6 cxd6 17 ♕c2

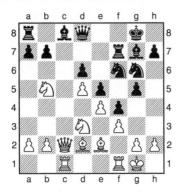

Position after 17 ♕c2
Black to move

Based on the pawn-break (i.e. playing c5), White has built up a strong attacking position on the queenside, while throwing in just one little defensive move on the other side of the board (12 f3). Black has replicated this strategy on the kingside by playing ...f5 also with the inclusion of just one defensive move (15...♖f7, intended to provide the c7-square with some extra cover). But now Black faces a very difficult and highly principled choice: should he continue 17...♘e8, another defensive move to prevent White from transferring a knight to c7 and thus cutting deeply into his queenside? Or should he take advantage of the opportunity provided by White's previous move (17 ♕c2, relinquishing control over the g4-square) and play 17...g4, which is a very attractive attacking move indeed for Black?

Chess art: You can do more than play chess on a chessboard! *Chess problems* and *endgame studies* are composed positions, designed to be artistic, instructive or pleasing in some way. There is generally a unique solution and a specific theme. You can find books and websites devoted to both. There are also solving contests.

And that is only the beginning of the complications. Should play continue 17...g4 18 ♘c7, the next question, of similar magnitude and complexity, arises.

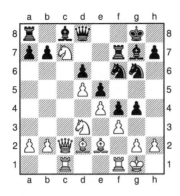

Position after 18 ♘c7
Black to move

Should Black now bring his rook into safety or can he burn all bridges behind him and lash out with 18...gxf3 19 gxf3 ♗h3 instead? And supposing Black chooses the latter, should White then accept the sacrifice (20 ♘xa8) or is an attempt to throw a spanner in the works by playing 20 ♘e6 the better choice?

These are mind-boggling questions, not just for a beginner but for any player, however advanced. And to think that, although we have made no fewer than twenty moves, we are still not 'out of book'!

It goes without saying that these moves and these questions far exceed the level of a learner's guide to chess, but I have included them because they may give the reader a glimpse of how accomplished a player he may *become*! They also provide a nice example of how invisible the division between opening and middlegame can be. One could even argue that there never really *was* an opening in this game, that it was typical middlegame choices, strategic at first, tactical later, right from the start. But the main reason why I have given this example is that it shows how all-important pawn-structure is in determining the course of a game. The pawns move into battle first. The pieces do no more than make use of the space created for them by their pawns.

Exercises

19) Let us take another look at the Queen's Gambit Accepted. Suppose that after 1 d4 d5 2 c4 dxc4 White plays 3 e3, attacking c4 with his king's bishop, and Black tries to consolidate his extra pawn by playing 3...b5 4 a4 c6 5 axb5 cxb5.

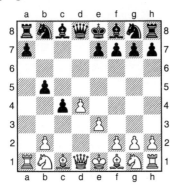

Position after 5...cxb5
White to move

How does White then gain a significant material advantage?

20) One of Black's options in the Benoni Defence (1 d4 ♘f6 2 c4 c5 3 d5) is to play 3...e5, the Czech Benoni. After 4 ♘c3 d6 5 e4, the position becomes even more closed than in the King's Indian game that we have just looked at.

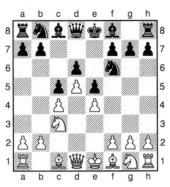

Position after 5 e4
Black to move

On what pawn-breaks should both sides base their long-term plans in this position?

21) Another long theoretical variation of the King's Indian Defence starts with 1 d4 ♘f6 2 c4 g6 3 ♘f3 ♗g7 4 g3 0-0 5 ♗g2 d6 6 0-0 ♘c6 7 ♘c3 a6 8 d5 ♘a5 9 ♘d2 c5 10 ♕c2 ♖b8 11 b3 b5 12 ♗b2.

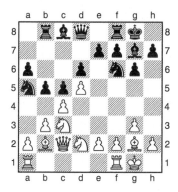

Position after 12 ♗b2
Black to move

Black has been the first to take the initiative, using his b-pawn as a battering-ram against White's queenside. Suppose that he were to open a second front in the centre by playing 12...e5, what strategic decision would White then have to make?

Anatoly Karpov and Garry Kasparov
The era of Soviet domination in chess lasted from the 1940s to the 1990s (except for Fischer's brief interruption). Anatoly Karpov (born in 1951) and Garry Kasparov (1963) were its last two great champions, between them dominating international chess throughout the late 1970s, 1980s and the 1990s. Karpov was World Champion from 1975 until 1985, when he was defeated by Kasparov in what was just one of no fewer than five matches they were destined to play for the highest title. The final years of Kasparov's reign were marred by great turmoil after Kasparov decided to break from FIDE in 1993 and start a rival chess organization. Kasparov was still widely seen as the world's best until his retirement in 2005, although he lost even 'his' version of the world title to Vladimir Kramnik in 2000.

Lesson 8: The Endgame

In the previous lesson we saw White follow the plan of opening a file and then using that file for an attack. The dirty work was done by White's c-pawn, which marched from c2 to c5 and captured a neighbouring pawn on d6 before perishing there. The c-file was then open for queen and rook to exert pressure on Black's position. We will use the same example one more time, now to illustrate an important difference between middlegame and endgame.

In the middlegame position from Lesson 7, although White had control over the c-file, Black had plenty of defenders to stop White from invading his position. In an endgame with just a rook each, dominance over the only open file can prove a decisive advantage.

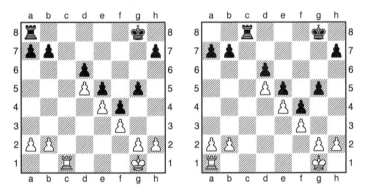

If in the left-hand position White is to move, he simply plays 1 ♖c7, attacking b7, threatening 2 ♖d7 and confining Black's king to the back rank all at the same time. If it is Black's turn to move, he can do nothing to stop White from playing 2 ♖c7, but he can ward off the immediate danger to his position by playing 1...♖f8 in order to meet 2 ♖c7 with 2...♖f7 (and then 3 ♖c8+ ♖f8).

If it is Black who controls the c-file, as in the right-hand diagram, then he has the advantage. After 1...♖c2, White finds himself with his back against the wall. If White is to move, he can still defend with 1 ♖f1 ♖c2 2 ♖f2.

The term 'advantage' denotes a situation where the side that 'holds the advantage' has the best chances of winning. This assessment might be due to him having more material than his opponent, or positional factors being in his favour, or a combination of the two. Note that any advantage, however big, can be ruined with a single blunder or with a series of bad moves, so there is never anything truly permanent about a positional evaluation.

The previous example makes it clear that control over the only open file is vital in evaluating any position, but especially in an endgame with rooks, i.e. a 'rook endgame'. But what if there are so few pawns left that the rooks roam freely over the entire board and the concept of open files becomes meaningless?

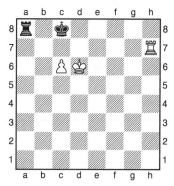

Even if all files are open, there can still be a marked difference in the *activity* of the rooks. In this position, White has the advantage because he still has a pawn (with the potential of becoming a queen!) while his opponent has none. So the question of how to evaluate this endgame is reduced to two options: either White is winning or it is a draw. The deciding factor in such endgames is usually the placement of king and rook. *Which side has the more active pieces?*

Many of these endgame positions have been studied and examined very carefully in the past, the result being an 'endgame literature' that is only slightly less voluminous than 'opening literature', though of a more lasting nature since endgame knowledge changes more slowly. If in a particular endgame position White has been proved to win, then that is the end of the story. In an endgame that has been exhaustively examined, there is no room for new discoveries, while in opening

theory the scope is endless. All that many players are interested in
when studying openings is finding a 'new move', in order to get their
opponents on unfamiliar (and hopefully unfavourable) ground.

In endgames there *are* no new moves, so understanding a position
is everything. In this respect much can be learned from a good endgame book. For those who are completely new to the game, the study
of endgames is unlikely to be their first priority; it is probably *getting*
to an endgame that they are worried about. Still, a few basic guidelines never go amiss. We will start in this simple rook endgame
where the situation is pretty clear.

Black's king stands with its back against the wall on c8, yet it does
block White's pawn. This is of crucial importance in an endgame
like this where everything hinges on whether the only remaining
pawn is able to queen. With White to move, everything is perfectly
simple: 1 ♖h8# is mate in one. But with Black to move, matters are
more complicated, for Black can play 1...♔b8, stepping out of the
mating-net while staying close enough to the white pawn to prevent
it from queening after 2 c7+? ♔b7!. For this reason White should
play not the immediate 2 c7+?, but 2 ♖h8+! driving the black king
further away. 2...♔a7 is forced and then, after the exchange of rooks
(3 ♖xa8+ ♔xa8) it is finally safe to play 4 c7 because 4...♔b7 can
now be met by 5 ♔d7! covering the promotion square (c8), and thus
making all further resistance useless.

But with Black's rook more actively placed, ready to join in the
battle, Black can draw.

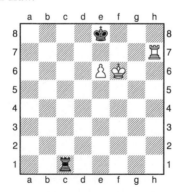

If it is White to move then of course 1 ♖h8# is still mate. But if it is
Black to move, he can now play 1...♖f1+. This chases White's king

away from f6, where it posed a deathly threat to Black's king *and* supported the e-pawn in its quest for promotion. In fact Black will go on checking White's king from behind until it drops back far enough to attack the rook, stopping the checks. But with the king away on a mission of its own, the pawn becomes vulnerable. Thus after 2 ♔e5 Black will play 2...♖e1+. If then 3 ♔d6 (threatening mate again with 4 ♖h8#) there is another check, 3...♖d1+, forcing the white king back yet again. A plausible sequel would be 4 ♔c5 ♖c1+ 5 ♔d4 ♖d1+ 6 ♔c3, when the checks cannot continue much longer, but now Black simply attacks the pawn by 6...♖d6! (or 6...♖e1!) 7 ♖h6 ♔e7, with a clear draw.

So in this type of endgame everything depends on the exact circumstances and on whose move it is.

Whether it concerns rooks, queens, bishops or knights, a thorough investigation of every endgame of the 'one piece each' type begins with the question: under what circumstances is one pawn against none enough to win? The conclusions reached form the starting point for a much deeper investigation of the more complex positions, such as two pawns against none, one against one and so on. Eventually, by adding more and more material, even such apparently simple endgames will become as complicated as middlegame positions.

The most basic endgame of all is king and pawn against king. Let us take a closer look at a few crucial positions.

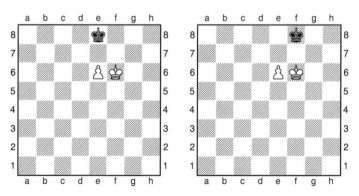

In pawn endings the first (and often the only) relevant aspect of a position is the question of whose move it is. Surprisingly perhaps, it is not always an advantage to move first. We have already encountered the term 'zugzwang' in Chapter 5. This motif is of enormous importance in all types of endings but nowhere more so than in pawn endgames.

If it is White to move in the left-hand position on the previous page, things are simple and straightforward. White plays 1 e7 and Black is in zugzwang. He *has* to move and 1...♔d7 is the only possibility. This allows White to play 2 ♔f7, taking control of e8 and ensuring the promotion of his pawn. We have already encountered this manoeuvre in the preceding rook endgame, an excellent illustration of how relevant pawn endgames are to all other types of endgames.

If Black is to move, he draws, but only if he plays 1...♔f8! (1...♔d8? loses – again – to 2 ♔f7!), reaching the position in the right-hand diagram.

If now 2 e7+ the king returns with 2...♔e8, when it may *look* like we have the identical position from the previous diagram after 1 e7, but there is the crucial difference that it is now White to move, not Black. The result is disastrous (from White's point of view): he has a choice between letting go of his pawn and playing 3 ♔e6, which is stalemate.

Things become more interesting if White plays a king move instead of 2 e7+, for instance 2 ♔e5. Now, if Black wants to keep using the stalemate motif, he has to make sure that he can play ...♔f8 again whenever White's king returns to f6 *and* that he can do exactly the same on the other side of the pawn: if White's king shows up at d6 Black *must* be able to play ...♔d8.

Once this mechanism is properly understood the defence is not too difficult, but any mistake will be fatal: 2...♔e7 3 ♔f5 ♔e8! (not 3...♔f8? 4 ♔f6! and White wins) 4 ♔e4 ♔e7 5 ♔e5.

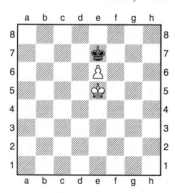

Position after 5 ♔e5
Black to move

Now 5...♔e8! is the only move to save the game. 5...♔f8? loses to 6 ♔f6! as does 5...♔d8? to 6 ♔d6!. But after 5...♔e8! White cannot make progress: 6 ♔f6 is met by 6...♔f8 and 6 ♔d6 by 6...♔d8. This special type of zugzwang, where two kings face each other with only one square in between them, is called the *opposition*. The player *not* having to move is said to 'have the opposition'. If Black is to move, he has to give way to White's pawn. With White to move, he can do no better than stalemate or retreat the king and try again, which, providing Black continues to defend well, is likely to result in a draw by threefold repetition within a few moves.

This motif is crucial to many pawn endgame positions. In the next diagram, for instance, if White is to move, he wins easily by just pushing his pawn:

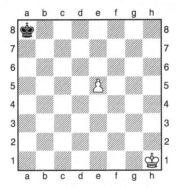

After 1 e6, the black king is too far away to stop the pawn (1...♔b7 2 e7 ♔c7 3 e8♕). But if it is Black to move, we are basically back in the previous diagram after 1...♔b7 2 ♔g2 (2 e6 now just loses the pawn after 2...♔c7 3 e7 ♔d7) 2...♔c6 3 ♔f3 ♔d5 4 ♔f4 ♔e6 5 ♔e4. If Black has firmly grasped the working of the opposition he will hold a draw here without any trouble.

Exercises

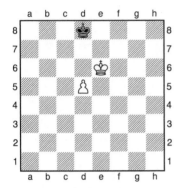

22) An exercise in making use of the opposition. White to play and win.

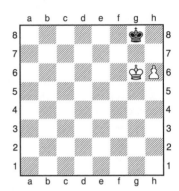

23) Black to move. White has the opposition so one might expect him to be winning. However, rook's pawns are different. Why is this position a draw?

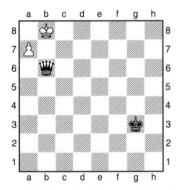

24) Another characteristic of rook's pawns is that they can sometimes draw against a queen! White is in check. It is easy to see that 1 ♔c8? loses to 1...♛xa7. But after 1 ♔a8 the situation is totally different. Why?

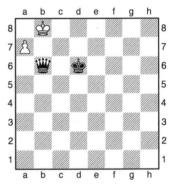

25) But this drawing mechanism does not always work. Can you see why in this position the proximity of Black's king makes a big difference?

Lesson 9: What's Next?

We have come to the end of this short introduction to the rules, the basic guidelines and – hopefully – the joys of chess. Anyone wishing to study the game in more detail should now have the basic vocabulary and the elementary knowledge to enable them to read and understand some of the more advanced and specialized books on chess, of which there are many. In fact the whole of chess history, its wisdom and culture have been documented in a vast literature that is being added to almost daily, especially if one includes websites. There are general instructive works, specialized books on openings, middlegames and endgames, (auto)biographies of many of the greatest players of all time and there are tournament books, documenting (and often commenting upon) all games that were played in a major tournament. All of these books are of interest in their own way and anyone attracted to books at all will quickly develop their own preferences in this field.

But if your primary aim is to improve your level of play, my first advice to you would be simply to start playing. You can find yourself a chess-playing friend, a neighbour or a local chess club and there are also many websites where you can play at any time and against any level of opposition. Playing is the best way to learn and above all to really integrate what you have learned. It is also the best way to find out if you really like chess or not. After all, chess should be a fun game, rather than a chore!

And if you happen to be one of those people who truly feel the fascination of chess, its mysteries and its logic, the lure of the brilliant moves that great players keep astonishing us with, you are surely destined to become a genuine chess lover. And for a chess lover the world does not have to be bigger than the 64 squares of a chessboard, at least not for the duration of a game. A board consisting of 8 x 8 squares of alternating dark and light colour with 32 chess pieces on it... This may not seem much, but for a chess-player it is enough.

I wish you good luck and a lot of fun in your further exploration of the world of chess.

Solutions

1) If it is White to move, he has a choice between advancing his pawn one square or capturing Black's pawn. If Black is to move, he has exactly the same options: he can either advance his pawn or capture White's pawn.

2) No, he can't. Capturing a pawn *en passant* is only allowed when that pawn has just left its original square by moving two squares forward and never at any later stage.

3) No. The white king is in check. White can either move his king or he can capture the black queen with his rook, but when the king is in check, castling is never allowed.

4) Yes and no. Castling *kingside* is not allowed, for the white king would then pass through a square where he would be in check from the black bishop. But castling *queenside* is allowed. It is true that the rook would then pass through a square where it would be under attack from the black bishop, but this is not a problem.

5) Black is not checkmated yet, for he can get out of the check by moving his pawn two squares forward. If White then captures that pawn with his queen though it really is checkmate. The black king has no squares and his two remaining pieces can do nothing to block the check. In fact, Black would be better off without at least one of them, for in that case his king would have an empty square that he could move to.

6) If it is White to move, it is stalemate. White's king has no legal moves, while his only remaining pawn is blocked and therefore cannot move either.

7) Both 3 ♕f3 and 3 ♕h5 threaten mate in one. Should Black overlook this threat and continue with an unsuspecting move like

3...♘c6??, then 4 ♕xf7# is mate. The game is over after just four moves! If Black *does* notice the threat, he can easily parry it by playing 3...♘f6 against 3 ♕f3 (but this does not work against 3 ♕h5) and by 3...♕e7 or 3...♕f6 against 3 ♕h5. In the latter case it is then White who has to be careful for Black is threatening 4...♕xf2+. This mate on f7 (or f2) is sometimes called Scholar's Mate. It is an opening trap which has found countless victims among generations of novices. Don't tell me you haven't been warned!

8) 1...♖xa2?? is a blunder because it allows White to play 2 ♖c8+, when 2...♗d8 (the only move, but it merely delays the inevitable) 3 ♖xd8# is checkmate. This is called a 'back-rank mate', because, apart from the action of White's rook, it is Black's king being closed in on the back rank by his own pawns that is his undoing. The simple creation of an escape-route by 1...h5, for example, would have prevented the mate and left Black with a solid material advantage.

9) White can indeed play the rather spectacular-looking move 1 ♘c3. This is made possible by two different pins, the one against Black's king which prevents the knight on e4 from moving at all and the one against Black's queen which leaves the queen on d5 unprotected in case Black plays 1...dxc3?? (allowing 2 ♕xd5). Black has in fact no choice but to move his queen away from d5 (e.g. 1...♕a5), allowing White to capture the knight on e4, thus reducing his material deficit to just one pawn.

10) The best move is without a shadow of a doubt 1 ♕xg7#! Another 'good' move is 1 ♕xd7, which wins a queen, but ... the game continues.

11) The mate in two is 1 ♗b3+ ♔h8 (forced) 2 ♗c3#. Again, like in some previous positions, White needs to be aware of the danger of stalemate. If, for example, White overlooks the mating move 2 ♗c3# and makes another move with the same bishop instead, the black king is stalemated on h8 and the game is drawn.

12) If Black goes the wrong way (1...♔h8??) he gets mated by 2 ♘f7#, but if the king moves away from the corner (1...♔f8!) White cannot win. He can *try*, and it is partly for this very ending that the fifty-move rule was invented, but if Black keeps finding the right

moves (and it is really only with his king in one of the corners that there ever can be a realistic chance of getting checkmated) he will be able to claim a draw after the 'ordeal' has lasted fifty moves.

13) White has a mate in two in this position with 1 ♘h6+! ♚h8 2 ♗c3#. The point of the winning procedure is to trap the enemy king in a corner square *of the same colour as the bishop* (a1 or h8 in this example); otherwise Black will always be able to escape. This takes considerable time and good technique (i.e. White has to know exactly what he is doing). In practice this endgame often ends in a draw (the fifty-move rule!) because White simply isn't able to work out the winning technique over the board.

14) 1 ♘f6+! forces Black to play either 1...♚g7 or 1...♚h8, when 2 ♘e4+ is at the same a check *and* an attack on Black's queen, making 3 ♘xd2 on the next move unavoidable. A move like 2 ♘e4+ is called a *discovered check*. The knight from f6 moves and by doing so it clears the e5-h8 diagonal for the bishop so that Black's king suddenly finds itself in check from the bishop. Since Black has to get out of the check, he is unable to do anything about the attack on his queen.

15) 1 ♖xf6+! wins the queen since, however Black recaptures on f6, his queen on d7 is left unprotected and will be lost on the next move (2 ♕xd7). White sacrifices an exchange (a rook for a knight) and this sacrifice pays off a huge dividend immediately. Please note, however, that this combination works only because the first move is a check! Had Black's king stood on h7 (instead of on g6) 1 ♖xf6? would not have been check and Black would have coolly replied 1...♕xc8, turning White's combination into a fiasco.

16) By playing 1 ♘g6+!! White forces his opponent to play 1...hxg6, 'half-opening' the h-file, when all White needs to do is to open his own half of the same file with 2 hxg3+! and it is mate (well, after 2...♕h4 3 ♖xh4# it is). Note that 2 hxg3+ is again a discovered check.

17) The spectacular queen sacrifice 1...♕g1+!! wins on the spot. 2 ♖xg1 is forced, but this allows 2...♘f2#! This is called a *smothered mate*. It is the knight that mates, but only because the king is unable to move, being surrounded (or 'smothered') by his own pieces.

18) 1 ♘e6++! wins. This is a *double check*, a check by two pieces simultaneously (and thus the symbol '++'). Black cannot reply 1...♗xf2+ since this would still leave his king in check from the knight. He *has* to move his king, thus allowing 2 ♘xd4 on the next move. Bishop captured, pin against f2 broken: White remains a piece to the good.

19) By playing 6 ♕f3! White attacks the rook on a8. Black is powerless to save it: the rook can't move and there is no way to protect it. Relatively best is 6...♘c6, which 'only' loses a knight after 7 ♕xc6+ ♗d7.

20) White's strategy should be to attack either on the queenside with b4 or on the kingside with f4. Black's future lies mainly in play on the kingside, based on ...f5, while he may also get the chance to lash out on the other side of the board with ...a6 followed by ...b5.

21) After 12...e5 White faces a strategic choice between opening the centre by capturing *en passant* on e6 or keeping the pawn-structure as it is: closed. In the former case White is likely to concentrate his forces on the 'backward' pawn on d6, a plan that quickly becomes concrete in the variation 13 dxe6 fxe6 14 cxb5 axb5 15 ♘ce4 followed by ♖ad1 at some point. If White refrains from capturing on e6, he is likely to initiate an attack on the kingside based on e4 (or e3) followed by f4. Which is the better plan is almost impossible to say with any degree of objectivity; it really is 'a matter of taste'.

22) White wins by taking the opposition: 1 ♔d6!, forcing the black king to move aside. If 1...♔e8 White plays 2 ♔c7!, freeing the way for his pawn through to d8. If 1...♔c8 White plays 2 ♔e7! with exactly the same consequences. The idea of blocking your own pawn is a paradoxical one, but in this situation it is the only way to win. If 1 d6? Black takes the opposition himself: 1...♔e8! and it is a draw as we have seen earlier. The opposition is the key to understanding this type of endgame.

23) Black draws by playing 1...♔h8! (if 1...♔f8? then after 2 h7! the pawn cannot be stopped). The difference between a rook's pawn and all other pawns comes to light after the logical 2 h7, for it is now not zugzwang but stalemate!

24) After 1 ♔a8 there is no win for Black because of the stale-mate motif. A queen cannot force a checkmate without the assistance of 'her' king so Black would have to move his king closer to a8, but if 1...♔f4 it is stalemate. This means that the queen will have to let the white king escape from a8 first, but after, for example, 1...♛a6 2 ♔b8 the threat of 3 a8♛ forces Black to drive the white king back in front of his pawn again (e.g. 2...♛b6+ 3 ♔a8), which brings us back where we started. White cannot make progress.

25) With Black's king so close to the promotion square, the picture is drastically changed. If now 1 ♔a8 Black uses the proximity of his king to create a mating-net: 1...♛c6+ 2 ♔b8 ♛c7+! 3 ♔a8 ♛c8#.

Magnus Carlsen
The current World Champion is Magnus Carlsen from Norway. Born in 1990, he first rose to prominence in January 2004, when he scored an outstanding 10½/13 in the C-group of the Wijk aan Zee tournament as a 13-year-old. Within a few months of this breakthrough he had already secured the title of International Grandmaster, one of the youngest players ever to do so. He smoothly progressed to world top level and from about 2010 onwards he was considered the best player in the world by many, though he did not obtain the official title of World Champion until he defeated Vishy Anand in a match in 2013. Carlsen is a true exponent of 21st-century chess as he embraces his role of media star and by being equally good in all time-limits: classical, blitz and rapid chess.

Useful Websites

There are many websites with good chess content and information. They are constantly changing, so be prepared to use a web search such as Google or Bing. Many of these sites feature links to other chess sites, so you will never be short of online chess resources.

chessclub.com – the Internet Chess Club (ICC), where you can play, watch events and find coaching
chess24.com – live chess and online play; much premium content
chessbase.com – the news site of a major chess software company
chess.com (including **chessvibes.com**) – a huge chess site with news, forums, contests, articles, etc.
2700chess.com – focuses on elite events, with a live rating list
chessdom.com – wide-ranging site with an international focus
chess-news.ru/en – a Russian chess news site
chess-calendar.eu – a detailed calendar of chess events
theweekinchess.com – news site with a weekly game download
chesspub.com – discussion forum with an emphasis on openings
playchess.com – ChessBase's online play site
uschess.org – USA chess federation
englishchess.org.uk – English chess federation
fide.com – World chess federation (+ links to national federations)
saintlouischessclub.org – home of the US championship
wikipedia.org/wiki/Chess – a lot of good chess content
youtube.com – there are many chess youtubers
iccf.com – international correspondence chess
chessprogramming.wikispaces.com – detailed information
stockfishchess.org – a leading freeware chess engine
theproblemist.org – composed chess problems
arves.org – endgame studies
paulvandersterren.nl – the author's web site
Notable chess tweeters: @MagnusCarlsen @GMHikaru @vishy64theking @Vachier_Lagrave @anishgiri

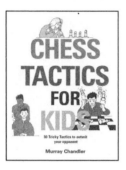
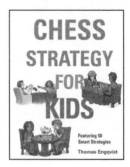
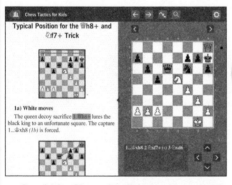